JAY DICKMAN

Our Inviting
Eastern Parklands

From Acadia to the Everglades

JOHN SHAW

Prepared by the Book Division
National Geographic Society, Washington, D. C.

Our Inviting Eastern Parklands:
From Acadia to the Everglades

Contributing Authors: Toni Eugene, Tom Melham,
  Scott Thybony, Jennifer C. Urquhart, Mel White
Contributing Photographers: Chip Clark, Jay Dickman,
  David Doubilet, Raymond Gehman, Chris Johns

Published by The National Geographic Society
Reg Murphy,
  President and Chief Executive Officer
Gilbert M. Grosvenor, *Chairman of the Board*
Nina D. Hoffman, *Senior Vice President*

Prepared by The Book Division
William R. Gray, *Vice President and Director*
Charles Kogod, *Assistant Director*
Barbara A. Payne,
  Editorial Director and Managing Editor

Staff for this book
John G. Agnone, *Project Editor and Illustrations Editor*
Jane H. Buxton, *Text Editor*
Suez B. Kehl, *Art Director*
Victoria Garrett Jones, Melanie Patt-Corner,
  Researchers
Mary B. Dickinson, Ron Fisher, *Consulting Editors*
Carl Mehler, *Map Editor*
Larry Camp, Joseph F. Ochlak, *Map Researchers*
Lewis R. Bassford, *Production Project Manager*
Timothy H. Ewing, Richard S. Wain, *Production*
Artemis S. Lampathakis, Meredith C. Wilcox,
  Illustrations Assistants
Sandra F. Lotterman, *Editorial Assistant*
Karen F. Edwards, Elizabeth G. Jevons,
  Peggy J. Oxford, *Staff Assistants*

Manufacturing and Quality Management
George V. White, *Director*
John T. Dunn, *Associate Director*
Vincent P. Ryan, *Manager*
R. Gary Colbert

Elisabeth MacRae-Bobynskyj, *Indexer*

RIGHT: *Near St. John's verdant hills, a family of
snorkelers takes in the undersea attractions of Virgin
Islands National Park.*
PAGE 1: *Appalachian fall brightens slopes of the Blue
Ridge Mountains in Shenandoah National Park.*
PAGES 2-3: *Clear waters of the Little Pigeon River flow
from the Great Smoky Mountains, joining 2,000 miles
of tree-lined streams within the national park.*

DAVID DOUBILET

Foreword
9

Acadia National Park
10

Mammoth Cave National Park
46

Great Smoky Mountains & Shenandoah National Parks
56

Biscayne National Park
104

Everglades National Park
112

Dry Tortugas National Park
150

Virgin Islands National Park
158

Notes on Contributors, Acknowledgments,
Additional Reading   197

Index   198

Key to Park Symbols   200

Foreword

by Bruce Babbitt, Secretary of the Interior

LIKE SO MANY OTHERS raised in the vast and open areas of the American West, I never bothered to explore the eastern parks. I sensed that any parks worth seeing—those with the most splendid mountains, the wildest rivers, and the most glorious landscapes— were all in the West. It's an assumption common among Westerners. It also happens to be wrong.

It wasn't until becoming Secretary of the Interior that I began to discover the extraordinary beauty of the eastern national parks. My introduction began on a spring backpacking trip with my son in Shenandoah National Park. We hiked trails painted bright with azaleas, past fields of grazing deer, made our way along rocky ridges and down the western slope. As a rattlesnake slithered beneath a rock, I was reminded that these parks are in fact wild. We made camp along a stream at the very bottom of the mountains, hanging our packs in trees to keep them away from bears. On our climb back, I was reminded that this was a real mountain.

I've also come to know one of the great unknown gems of the entire system: the Dry Tortugas. Several hours by boat from Key West, we enjoyed a magical weekend fishing and watching an extraordinary display of nesting birds. Magnificent frigate birds, with their bright red ballooning throats, perched in trees; sooty terns, built so perfectly for flight, canvassed the beaches.

At Great Smoky Mountains, I was struck by the great biodiversity of the mixed hardwood forests. Only 50 years ago, both Great Smokies and Shenandoah were quite devastated, cutover areas. With five decades of National Park Service care, these lands have recovered and now stand among our great rugged, wild parklands. Many of the eastern parks are magnificent testaments to the restorative powers of both nature and humans.

There is wild country and great beauty in the eastern national parks, and in a region so densely populated they play an important role. Throughout the world, we see each day new evidence of an ecological collapse. Our best hope for reversing this devastating trend is to impart a conservation ethic, to change our consumption habits, and to explore methods of living more lightly on the land. What better place to begin that process than in our national parks?

These eastern parks are a window through which millions of Americans can renew their connection to the natural world. They are the places where this educational process begins most easily— where the natural balance is so obvious and invigorating. They are the natural first step toward a new American environmental ethic.

So read on. And then go visit.

Great egret in Everglades National Park preens the elegant breeding plumage that almost brought its kind to extinction at the turn of this century. The need to protect such birds and other animals in South Florida propelled establishment of the park in 1947. Changes outside park boundaries continue to threaten the preserve's wildlife and environmental balance.

CHRIS JOHNS

Acadia National Park

by Mel White • Photographed by Raymond Gehman

Parkland shares Maine's Mount Desert Island with villages where fishing and shipbuilding traditions endure; at Seal Harbor, lobster boats and pleasure craft wait in the morning fog.

tanding 1,530 feet above Maine's rocky shore, Cadillac Mountain is not only the highest peak in Acadia National Park, but also the highest point on the Atlantic coastline of North America. Choose the right morning to drive to the top, and you could be the first person on the continent to see the rays of the sun. If, afterward, you drop by the Bar Harbor Chamber of Commerce, they'll give you a card enrolling you in the Cadillac Mountain Sunrise Club—an association of which I, regrettably, am not a member.

I was right on time, the morning of my initiation; the sun was not. In the dark and the fog, huddled against the wind in a stark mountaintop landscape of bare rock, I felt like a moorland druid vainly waiting for some celestial omen. For a moment a pink line appeared above the horizon, and images formed in the leaden sea: islands like stepping-stones reaching out from the lights of town, and the slow red flash of a lighthouse. Then the fog closed in, and the world shrank to the size of a handball court.

Was I disappointed? Sure, a little…but hardly surprised. Fog is as basic to the Maine coast as barnacles and lobster buoys; without it the spruce and fern wouldn't grow so lush, and picturesque lighthouses would lose their romance. Fog is part of the package you get when you cross the causeway to Mount Desert Island.

I sought solace at my favorite Bar Harbor bakery—it's amazing what a tall stack of blueberry pancakes can do for the spirit. Before long I was winding back up the mountain again, to find the same prospect transformed under a luminous pale-blue sky.

The stark terrain took on a gentler look as I walked it in the light of day; Cadillac's flattish bald dome gleamed as smooth, pastel-pink granite, flecked with bits of black hornblende like pepper in a bisque. The same ancient rock forms the tops of Dorr and Champlain Mountains, a few hundred feet below. When Samuel de Champlain explored this coast in 1604, these treeless summits inspired his name *l'Isle des Monts-déserts*: the island of bare mountains.

The green stepping-stones of the Porcupine Islands pointed northeast toward the mainland across Frenchman Bay; as I watched, the M.V. *Bluenose* steamed past on its daily shuttle, ferrying passengers and vehicles to Nova Scotia. The blocky red-and-white Egg Rock lighthouse sat alone in the mouth of the bay, its duty done for a while. To the south, broad, low islands—Baker, Sutton, and Great and Little Cranberry—floated in the Atlantic like pieces of a jigsaw puzzle uncoupled from the ragged shore.

Looking north over Mount Desert I saw not just the hills, lakes, and forest of a national park, but also the highways, schools, a golf course, and, most prominently, the town of Bar Harbor strung along the shore below—a legacy of Acadia's beginnings shortly after the turn of the century. At a time when national parks were thought of as vast, untouched tracts in the West, this, the first national park east of the

Mississippi, was assembled not from public land with public funds but with private donations, one precious part at a time, on an island that was already an important tourist destination. Originally named Lafayette when established in 1919, it was renamed Acadia ten years later, when land on the Schoodic Peninsula was incorporated. Acadia now covers 30,000 acres of Mount Desert—a little less than half its area—plus 2,000 more on the Schoodic Peninsula (the lumpy ridgeline off to the east) and 3,000 on Isle au Haut, out of sight to the southwest. The interlacing of parkland and private property, and the sometimes competing values of preservation and tourism, have always challenged those who would protect the island's wild side.

"Acadia's problems are no different from those of any other national park," Duane Pierson, then president of Friends of Acadia, had told me one day in his Bar Harbor office. "It's just that here they're magnified many times." While Acadia is the fifth smallest national park in the country, it has the seventh highest visitation rate, receiving about 3 million visitors annually. Most people arrive en masse in the brief summer season, filling campgrounds, clogging roads, and leading some to wonder how much more popularity the park can take.

Duane was one of several people who described Acadia to me as a "10-to-4 park": full of visitors who cruise the designated scenic loop, drive up Cadillac for its singular picture-book panorama, and head back toward Cottage Street to buy T-shirts and carved puffins, thinking they've seen it all. That kind of traveler is in the majority at many parks, but here it seems especially sad. As Duane Pierson put it, "This has always been a place for the adventurous of soul." Today's Acadia is sometimes a crowded playground, yet corners of solitude still reward those who choose the quiet paths. But it's sad mostly because this is a park of endless discovery—of small wonders as well as grand vistas. Whether in daylight, or dark blue sky, or fog, it would be easier to fit the puzzle pieces of the Cranberry Islands back together again than to see all of Acadia from the top of Cadillac Mountain.

Just after another sunrise the wind was roaring through the birches around Witch Hole Pond. For all the bluster, there was no real threat—the warm dawn promised a good day for a walk south through the heart of Acadia. The gusts stirred the leaves, but they weren't as noisy as the squeak-scold of a fidgety red squirrel, the ubiquitous and indefatigable watchdog of the north woods. *Okay, okay, you spotted me,* I told him silently. *Do you have to wake up the whole neighborhood?*

No chance of that. I was up people-early, but hereabouts I ranked as a lazybones. Every spruce seemed to have a pair of nuthatches tootling like toy trumpets as they searched for breakfast. A snowshoe hare bolted from beside the path, and then, as they so often do, froze just at the edge of the trees to try to figure out my intentions. I raised my binoculars and watched his whiskers twitch, but I knew better than to think I could get closer. Two more steps and he'd have been gone.

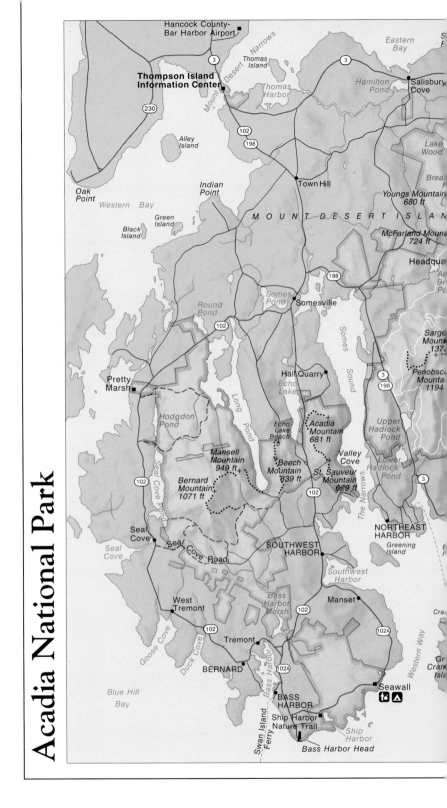

Acadia National Park

Here in early September, his brown fur showed no sign yet of the white coat he wears for camouflage in the winter snow.

Wildflowers were mostly past their season, but blue asters were still blooming, and white ones, and everywhere, goldenrod. At the

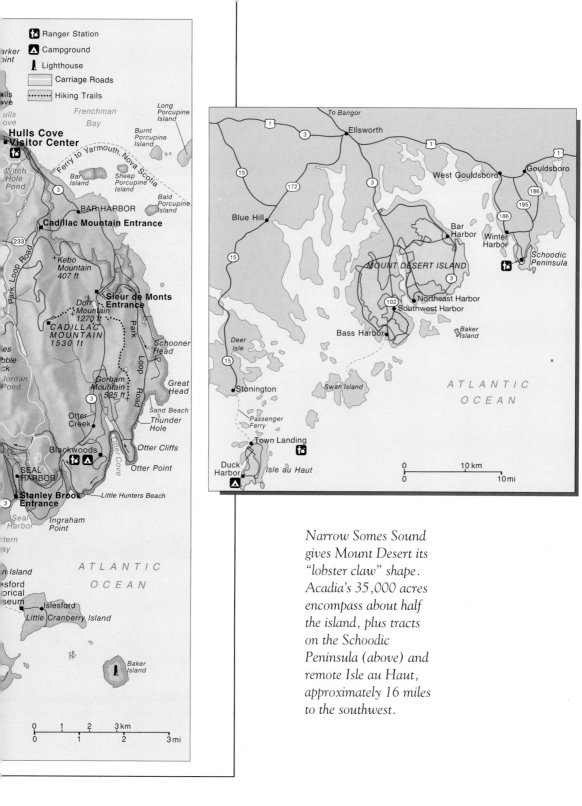

Narrow Somes Sound gives Mount Desert its "lobster claw" shape. Acadia's 35,000 acres encompass about half the island, plus tracts on the Schoodic Peninsula (above) and remote Isle au Haut, approximately 16 miles to the southwest.

Breakneck Ponds a flotilla of black ducks messed about near the edge of the water. I sneaked through the trees to try for a better look, but of course they saw me coming and swam edgily away. With a startling "graaak," a great blue heron laboriously flapped itself airborne and

Seal Harbor lobsterman Gordon King (opposite) bands the claws of his catch to keep aggressive tankmates from eating each other. Mostly dark green in their ocean home, lobsters turn orange-red (below) when cooked. The waters around Acadia yield a healthy share of Maine's $74 million annual harvest of the tasty crustacean.

MICHAEL MELFORD

landed atop a conical beaver lodge on the far shore. A tiny pied-billed grebe slipped beneath the surface with hardly a ripple. I moved away to leave them all in peace.

In another era, what I was doing here—poking along, watching birds, smelling flowers, and generally feeling grateful to be away from traffic and crowds—might have been called "rusticating." The seeds of today's park were planted in that frock-coated, silk-hatted time, and later nurtured by as unlikely a group of "rustics" as ever stopped to hear a robin sing.

In the mid-19th century, painters of the Hudson River school found in Mount Desert Island a rich source for the extravagantly dramatic landscapes that were all the rage then. Other travelers followed, spending summers in the homes of the farmers, fishermen, and shipbuilders who'd settled here. Not all were artists; many were simply refugees from burgeoning East Coast cities, enjoying a simpler life.

These rusticators, as they came to be called, were the first tricklings of a flood. By 1880, Mount Desert had 30 hotels; in 1887, the opulent *Boston and Mt. Desert Limited Express* began bringing trainloads of New England's elite. Soon, anyone with any pretension to the social register had a summer house on the island. The Vanderbilts, Astors, Carnegies, Morgans, Fords, and—most significantly, as it turned out—the Rockefellers built mansions they disingenuously called "cottages" along the shore, until the northeastern coast of Mount Desert was known as Millionaire's Row.

John D. Rockefeller, Jr., one of the cottagers, was to donate nearly 11,000 acres of his private estate to the growing park. Accompanying this monumental gift was another equally generous, for which countless visitors to Acadia have given thanks in the decades since.

Rockefeller believed—ironically enough, in light of the source of his fortune—that the motorcar would be the ruin of picturesque Mount Desert. Beginning in 1913 (the year Bar Harbor finally repealed its ban on the newfangled contraptions) he began planning a network of what he called "carriage roads" through some of the island's most beautiful areas. Originally designed for horse-drawn carriages, they welcome walkers, horseback riders, and bicyclers as well; automobiles were, and are, banned. Eventually 57 miles of these broad, smooth gravel paths were built; 50 are inside the park boundary today. Seventeen imposing stone bridges are scattered along the routes, each one designed for its particular setting.

Wilderness trails they're not, but Acadia's carriage roads are perfect for lazy, contemplative—rusticatory—strolls, appreciative of things too often overlooked: clustered bunchberries, brilliant crimson against dark green star moss; a big peach-colored caterpillar on the white bark of a paper birch; even the clicking of a squirrel's teeth, tearing the scales from a pinecone.

As I neared Eagle Lake I came upon a delicately patterned salamander, called a red-spotted newt, lying in the dusty road. Fearful for its future now that the speeding mountain bikers were out—they've become increasingly common, and controversial, in the park in recent years—I moved it to an adjoining marsh, drying now but still with a few white water lilies in bloom.

The wind had ripped the clouds apart; the clearing sky forecast a brilliant afternoon. To the south, more history was written on a hillside. A faint line, separating the darker trees above from the lighter ones below, marked the limit of a massive fire that roared across Mount Desert in 1947, blackening more than 17,000 acres. Where the fire burned, faster-growing deciduous trees like birch, aspen, and maple have grown back; spruce, fir, and hemlock, with their darker foliage, dominate in forests that were spared. The fire changed Mount Desert in another way, too: It destroyed most of the cottages on Millionaire's Row, bringing that opulent period to an end. The motels, cabins, and restaurants now lining State Route 3 near Bar Harbor replaced the mansions, as birch replaced spruce.

At the south end of Eagle Lake I left the carriage road for a trail that led me along the eastern shore of Jordan Pond, justly considered one of the park's prettiest bodies of water. From its southern end I looked back north on what may be Acadia's most famous view: The Bubbles (an obviously bowdlerized name for these symmetrical twin round hills) rising above Jordan Pond. Like much of the park's scenery, this striking vista owes its form to ice.

Glaciers have moved across New England many times in the past three million years, scouring and carving the landscape. In the most recent episode—between 100,000 and 18,000 years ago—the relentless ice created U-shaped valleys running north and south; one valley, Somes Sound, which nearly splits (Continued on page 29)

FOLLOWING PAGES: Bent but still standing, spruce trunks testify to the power of wind and waves where forest meets rocky seacoast near Otter Point.

Hikers on Cadillac
Mountain, the park's
highest point, overlook
Bar Harbor,
Frenchman Bay, and
Sheep Porcupine
Island. Treeless peaks
of pink granite inspired
explorer Samuel de

Champlain's name
l'Isle des Monts-déserts:
the island of bare
mountains. Long Pond
(opposite), seen from
Beech Mountain, fills a
depression gouged by
a glacier that retreated
18,000 years ago.

21

Green seaweed forms smoky patterns in the surf at Little Hunters Beach (opposite). Shiploads of wave-rounded cobblestones from Mount Desert Island paved 19th-century streets in Boston and other cities. The jumble of life in a tide pool, where snail-like periwinkles feed among the mussels and rockweed, contrasts with the simplicity of a pattern formed by fractured granite.

LARRY ULRICH (LEFT); GLENN VAN NIMWEGEN

Champlain ran aground on a ledge just off Otter Point (opposite) in 1604 and had to lay up ashore for repairs. On this exposed coast, low tide reveals algae-covered granite boulders, their contours smoothed by the relentless force of wind-driven waves (above). Finding food and shelter where none seems apparent, harebells bloom on a rock face near the park's Ocean Drive.

*Stripped of its green
cloak, the sinuous
skeleton of a spruce
(opposite) remains
an object of beauty.
Drooping hobblebush
branches (left)
sometimes take root
where their tips touch
the ground, tripping
passersby and giving
the plant its aptly
descriptive name.
June's white blooms on
a bunchberry (below),
a relative of dogwood,
will later yield
clusters of brilliant
scarlet fruits.*

GLENN VAN NIMWEGEN; TIM BLACK (RIGHT)

Mount Desert in two, is the only fjord on the United States' Atlantic coast. Glaciers gouged out other low places inland that later filled with water; Jordan Pond and Eagle Lake were formed in such a manner. Ice moving to the south created gradual slopes on the north sides of hills, while it "plucked" rock from south slopes, leaving them steep and rugged. The Bubbles show this effect clearly: From Jordan Pond their south faces are steeply pitched; from overlooks on the west side of Cadillac, they appear, almost unrecognizably, as long ridges.

On my way back north I made a quick side trip to the top of South Bubble to visit Bubble Rock, an 11-ton boulder at the very edge of a cliff, seemingly held in place only by a whimsical suspension of gravity. A classic example of a glacial erratic, Bubble Rock was picked up by a glacier 20 miles away, carried to this spot, and set in place when the ice melted. Despite its precarious position, Bubble Rock seems comfortable in its new home; after all, it moved there 18,000 years ago.

Trails at Acadia range from strolls along the park's famed carriage roads to strenuous hikes scaling mountain summits. Some visitors prefer to travel where no paths go at all. Protected by a safety line, a young participant in an outdoor-adventure program gets a taste of rock climbing near Thunder Hole.

Most of my Indian summer days at Acadia were cut from the same pattern: forebodingly gray and windy early, clearing to warm, sunny afternoons. Pretty soon I began to take this daily miracle for granted, like the tide and the "I Brake for Lobster" bumper stickers on RVs along Route 3. One morning, though, I woke to a stubborn drizzle that, while ebbing to mist now and then, showed no sign of breaking up. The hike I had planned was out—and that's when I got the idea that this might be excellent weather for a drive around the Park Loop Road.

Much of the concern about crowding and overuse at Acadia focuses on this popular 20-mile route along the southeastern coast of Mount Desert. In an effort to relieve congestion the park has made a 14-mile section one-way; but the summer traffic is still so bad that studies recommend substituting shuttle buses for private vehicles. For nearly a week I had put off making the drive; but on a day like this....

On a day like this, most people stay home and miss the way the soft light and rain put a springlike glow on the scenery. At the start of the loop, just north and west of Bar Harbor, mist glistened on birch bark, silvery against the rich green of the spruce. A ranger just setting up shop at the tollgate waved me on through.

I stopped briefly at Sand Beach, a place that would seem ordinary on many shores but stands out as an anomaly on this geologically young coast, where waves haven't had time to grind rock to sand. Here, much of the "sand" is the crushed shells of billions of whelks, periwinkles, crabs, sea urchins, and other marine creatures. Sand Beach is known as a swimming spot for vacationers so desperate for a romp in the surf that they'll brave its 55-degree water. (Mount Desert natives swim in inland lakes, where temperatures reach a more human range.) It was deserted today, as the wind piled up waves along the shore.

For the next two miles the loop road skirts the edge of the

Atlantic Ocean, through a landscape that generations of travelers have revered as the essence of Acadia. Here is the storied rockbound coast of Maine at its most beautiful; here an infinite succession of waves explode against granite infinite in form: huge, flat, stair-step slabs, jumbled broken blocks, and the sheer incised cliffs of Otter Point. The landscape architect Frederick Law Olmsted, Jr., who helped design this road in the 1930s, described the type of scenery appropriate for motorists as having "a certain bigness of sweep"—a peculiar phrase that seemed less odd as I spent more time on the coastline, and ended up stuck in my mind like a line from a song.

At nearby Thunder Hole I realized that I had more or less accidentally arrived at the perfect moment to see this celebrated Acadia attraction at its best. Waves working through the millennia have widened a crack in the rock here to a long rectangular opening, like a bathtub with one end missing; in heavy surf, the water compresses air in the hole, causing a low boom like distant thunder. WHOOMP, it goes, or, for a really big wave, whu-WHOOMP. The park warns visitors to prepare for disappointment on a calm day; this morning the sea was pounding, and Thunder Hole did not disappoint.

I stopped to watch from the stairs well above the seaside observation platform—not because of any prescience, but because that's where the few other people out this early were standing. I soon picked up the rhythm: a calm (and silent) period of three or four minutes followed by a series of big waves that smashed against the back of the hole, sending geysers of foam everywhere.

Before long a young couple arrived, during a lull in the waves; she hung back, but he obviously couldn't understand why everybody was so far from the action. He skipped down the steps and perched on the railing, camera cocked and ready.

A very pregnant pause followed, as the ocean caught its breath.... Whu-WHOOMP!

Well, all of us here were at least a little damp already.

Beyond Thunder Hole, the road quickly neared the formidable wall of Otter Cliffs. I pulled over and, hat jammed down on my brow, rock-hopped to the water's edge. I stood staring out to sea while the surf broke around me, the spume eddied away, and the wind blew the rain into my face—much in the attitude, I fantasized, of a true Down East native, oblivious to such trifles as foul weather. On calmer days I had sat on shore and watched loons dive and harbor seals stick their heads up to stare at me with big dark eyes before sliding back below the surface. None were to be seen today; only we hardy folk were out. Black-backed gulls tacked across the wind, and the little seabirds called black guillemots rode the swell like wooden toys. A painter determined to capture the power of this scene, the surging ocean and the cascading fountains of seawater on rock, could spend the better part of a lifetime here, and no doubt some have done just that. Bigness of sweep—exactly!

The drizzle stopped as the road turned inland again, past a carriage-road crossing and the lower end of Jordan Pond, where I had ended my hike a few days before. Today The Bubbles on the far shore were primly hidden behind opaque cottony mist. One of the park naturalists had told me that her favorite walk followed Jordan Stream, the pond's outlet, south toward Seal Harbor. I grabbed my pack and set out to see what she meant.

During this lull in the weather, in all-encompassing fog, the trail along the creek was supernaturally quiet. Ripples and small waterfalls trilled like flutes, and the hammering of a woodpecker carried as crisply as a snare drum. Jordan Stream's rocky runs punctuated still pools; the ferny woods had the boreal smell of spruce and fir.

Soon the path led me to a carriage-road intersection and Mr. Rockefeller's beautifully arched and buttressed Cobblestone Bridge. Built in 1917, it was the first Acadia bridge and the only one constructed of cobbles instead of hand-hewn granite. Of all the carriage-road bridges I saw, it seemed the most organic: From the streambed, I could almost believe that its stones accreted naturally here in this pretty valley, among the maple, hemlock, birch, and beech.

It was all too enchanted to last for long. As I headed back the mist lowered and turned to rain, this time a no-fooling steady shower; soon there was a constant trickle off my hat brim onto my parka. I was still a quarter-mile from the trailhead when I decided that, even for a hardy adopted son of Maine, it was beginning to look like a good day to buy a few T-shirts.

Fog and drizzle don't dampen the hopes of young fishermen perched on Otter Point. Though sometimes vexing to vacationers, the coast's abundant moisture nourishes Acadia's lush forests, ferns, and wildflowers.

"You've got to roll up your sleeves and get down on your stomach if you really want to see a tide pool." The offshore breeze had hardly carried away this earthy advice when park naturalist Heidi Doss demonstrated that there was nothing metaphorical about her choice of words: She shed her green parka and Smokey Bear hat and settled down by a shallow pool a few yards from the swirling surf, like a thirsty cowpoke at a desert water hole. Following Heidi's lead, all of us on her field trip were soon in the same posture.

We were at Ship Harbor, on the southwestern edge of Mount Desert, to learn about tide pools, the fragile and fascinating worlds where saltwater plants and animals live half their lives cut off from the ocean. On this part of the Maine coast, tides average around ten feet; with low tide just minutes away this morning, the retreating sea had left dozens of pools in the cracks and low places of the pink granite ledges around us. The living things in these tide pools must be both tenacious and adaptable: Summer sun can quickly raise the temperature of their microhabitats, and rainwater can dilute the salt content.

In the corner of the pool where I prostrated myself the limpid water was as cold as glacial melt. Heidi had told us that studying a tide pool was "like looking through a window at a rain forest," and, sure enough, I soon saw analogies between these two seemingly dissimilar ecosystems. Despite the profusion of life—rockweed, algae, and various filamentous unknowns competed with barnacles for space on every surface—it was easy to overlook the individuals living within.

As my perception adjusted to the Lilliputian scale of the pool, a brown patch of rock became a limpet, a mollusk with a cymbal-shaped flattened shell. In one of life's numberless adaptations here at the nexus of sea and land, every limpet has a "home" to which it returns after moving about to feed; the edge of its shell has grown to conform exactly to irregularities in the rock at this particular spot, sealing in moisture and keeping the animal from drying out at low tide.

The brown pebbles scattered everywhere in the pool were snail-like periwinkles, which glide over rocks, feeding on algae. I picked up an orange-size stone; under my ten-power hand lens, insignificant pieces of grit in its crevices were revealed as astonishingly tiny periwinkles. And surprise! Periwinkles have eyes—flat black buttons on the sides of their heads—and, just inboard, two feelers ("sensory tentacles," I later read) with which they seemed constantly to be checking the surface as they slid across the relatively huge expanse of rock. As I scanned farther with my lens I was mildly shocked to come across a translucent, multi-appendaged creature with an elongated head that looked remarkably like the monster from the movie *Alien*, miniaturized a thousand times. I carefully put the rock back and turned to another part of the pool.

By stirring the water near a patch of barnacles, I was able to fool a few of them into thinking that the tide was returning, whereupon they opened the top plates of their shells and began a rhythmic motion of their feathery legs, blindly scooping for microscopic food particles—this activity constituting the totality of their existence save for reproduction, which, in the case of these shrimplike crustaceans permanently cemented to the rock, is itself nothing to write home about.

Barnacles in their encrusted homes, immune to the buffeting of the strongest surf, seemed fortified against all dangers. But patiently crawling nearby was a relentless enemy, the dog whelk. Whelks, which look like streamlined periwinkles, drill into prey and feed on the soft tissue inside. Their color may depend on their food: Some were shades of gray, but others were a pretty butterscotch swirl.

I had just noticed a gray-green crab hiding in a niche in the rocks—it had been right beneath my nose the whole time—when someone nearby found a sea anemone, with ghostly pale arms that withdrew at a touch. Sea anemones have specialized organs called nematocysts, inside which coiled tubes wait to spring out and inject poison into prey and predator alike; in their jellyfish cousins these can be dangerous to humans, but the anemones' sting is too weak to be harmful. Heidi, sorting through seaweed in a low pool, came up with a sea star waiting for the returning tide to resume hunting. When the sea star finds its prey—a scallop or mussel, for instance—it uses its five arms to pull the shell apart, everts its stomach through its mouth, and digests its meal outside its own body.

In the midst of these diverse, and occasionally bizarre, creatures, I found myself with a feeling that I'd had before, in the forests of Costa Rica and Peru: that I could spend a very long time here before the pace of discovery slowed, that each layer of life concealed another even more complex. The naturalist Rachel Carson, who summered on the Maine coast, wrote in *The Edge of the Sea*: "Tide pools contain mysterious worlds within their depths, where all the beauty of the sea is subtly suggested and portrayed in miniature." Mystery, indeed—and beauty, too, for those with open minds and rolled-up sleeves.

At 7 a.m. the mail boat cast off lines and pulled away from the dock in the little fishing town of Stonington, where white frame houses crowded hillsides around the harbor. I zipped my parka against the chilly breeze and looked hopefully to the northwest; a strip of blue showed below another gray morning sky. We cruised seaward through a bay dotted with tiny islands, each wearing a butch haircut of spruce trees, as eider ducks and loons paddled beside us.

Soon more substantial terrain rose ahead: This was Samuel de Champlain's *Isle au Haut*, or "high island," today the remotest and least developed part of Acadia, 16 miles southwest of Mount Desert. Three thousand acres of parkland take up most of the southern half of Isle au Haut; the rest of the island is privately owned, with summer residences and a small year-round community. The only park facilities are a few campsites and primitive toilets, a hand-operated water pump, and 17 miles of hiking trails. The mail boat is the only way in or out.

"There's very little mention of Isle au Haut in Acadia literature and programs," ranger Kent Mattingly told me, "and that's not an oversight—that's by design. If people find it on their own, fine, but we're not going to encourage visitation." Only 50 people at a time are allowed in this part of the park all year round. The day I visited, the restrictions were hardly needed: One campsite was occupied, and one couple made the trip over with me.

After he had met the boat at Town Landing, Kent and I sat and talked awhile across a picnic table at the nearby ranger station. I mentioned the well-publicized—for Isle au Haut, anyway—cliffs at the southern tip of the island and discovered that a Cadillac-summit impulse operates even in this out-of-the-way place. "Too many people head straight for the cliffs because they've been told they must see them," Kent said. "But they miss a lot if they hurry. I enjoy the smaller things: lichens growing on a rock, or an arrangement of miniature spruces among the ferns. I grew up in California, and they remind me of the Japanese gardens I used to visit there. I believe these types of intimate scenes are among the most beautiful the island has to offer—especially after a rain, when the colors are wet and shining."

It had, in fact, rained the night before I visited Isle au Haut, and as I walked south through the open woodland I paused often at some of Kent's intimate scenes. I knelt on the damp ground to inspect a regiment of the red-topped lichen called British soldiers growing atop a stump. I stopped again for a close look at a shiny caramel-colored mushroom, just bursting through the needle-covered earth. The perfume of hay-scented fern, one of the headiest in nature, filled the air in a clearing; not sweet or flowery, and not exactly like hay, either, the smell is rich and green and, for me, always evocative of days and places like this.

At a bog filled with sphagnum moss, pitcher plants grew in scattered clumps; the blood-red veins of their hooded leaves gave them a macabre look appropriate for this insectivorous species. Along the edge I harvested some nicely fat red cranberries that the Isle au Haut critters had overlooked.

Somewhere overhead a raven croaked, and when I looked I saw, one more time, clouds vanishing out to sea. By the time I reached Merchant Cove, on the southeastern coast, the transformation was complete: Sunlight glinted off ripples in water as calm as I'd yet seen it. Why on earth, I wondered as I took off my sweater, had I brought a down vest?

I followed a path called the Goat Trail southwest along the shoreline, into the woods and out again to skirt cobblestone beaches. The whitish granite of Isle au Haut differs in origin from Mount Desert's pink stone, and in cliffy places the rocks shone in dazzling contrast to the blue ocean. As beautiful as the coast is near Otter Point, this seemed to me its superior. Time after time I stopped and thought, *This is the postcard I want to take home.*

Near Squeaker Cove I paused to watch a lobsterman hauling traps into his boat. The triangular fin of a harbor porpoise broke the surface between us, and then a second, and perhaps a third—I couldn't be sure as they staggered their appearances. I scrambled up a trailside boulder for a better look and watched until they disappeared to the east.

Is Isle au Haut really this magical, or was it just a chance combination of elements today? The glorious calm weather; the magnificent forest; the colors of sky and sea, rocks and trees…I hadn't seen a soul on the island in four hours of walking. It seemed my own private preserve, of the best this wild coast had to offer.

I found a smooth, sun-warmed rock near the waterline, dumped my pack, and sat down for lunch. *It's best to keep some perspective and objectivity now*, I thought. What else had Kent Mattingly told me? "I suppose my favorite trail," he said, "is whichever one I happen to be on at the time"—a little Oriental philosophy to go with his Japanese gardens.

In that spirit, I'm reluctant to do anything that would draw attention to the most unspoiled, unpeopled part of the park. I found my own

favorite Acadian spot right here, along the Goat Trail on Isle au Haut on a blue afternoon in September. Soon it would be time to hustle back along the path to catch the five o'clock ferry to the mainland. But I didn't want to leave just yet. The sandpipers I scared away had come back to teeter on the wave-splashed rocks below, and the eiders out in Deep Cove seemed to have gotten used to me, too. I wanted to stay just a little longer and enjoy the sunshine and the view. The lobsterman had finished his work; his boat was chugging around the headland, riding the flat line of the horizon. He probably couldn't see me sitting there on the rocks, but I waved good-bye anyway.

A sentinel raven keeps watch from its perch on the Schoodic Peninsula, a 2,000-acre tract of parkland across Frenchman Bay from Mount Desert Island. As poisonous as they are attractive, golden-hued fly amanita mushrooms spring up throughout Acadia's woodlands after summer rains. Their even more deadly relative, the destroying angel, also grows in the park.

The Abnaki Indians called Mount Desert Island "Pemetic": the sloping land. A low mountain at the southern end of Eagle Lake (left) takes that name today. Twin hills known as The Bubbles command the view across Jordan Pond, where newlyweds relax on the lawn of a popular park restaurant. Less conspicuous but just as lovely, a rain-spangled wild rose blooms amid overarching grass.

When fall comes
to Acadia, red maple
(opposite) lives up to
its name; pale birch
bark makes a fitting
backdrop for foliage
that varies from pale
yellow to brightest
crimson. Deciduous
trees dominate sections
of the park burned in a
catastrophic 1947 fire.
A brooklet (right)
cascades down
stone ledges on
Cadillac Mountain.

FOLLOWING PAGES:
Braving water that
averages only 55°F
in midsummer, visitors
enjoy a sunny day
at Sand Beach. Rare on
the rocky, geologically
young Maine coast,
the "sand" here consists
mostly of the crushed
shells of countless
sea creatures.

Visiting Acadia

MAINE
ESTABLISHED: February 26, 1919
SIZE: 35,000 acres
HEADQUARTERS
P. O. Box 177, Bar Harbor, Maine 04609
Phone (207) 288-3338

HOW TO GET THERE
From Ellsworth drive 18 miles south on Me. 3 to Mt. Desert Island, where most of the park is located; the Visitor Center is also on Mt. Desert Island, about three miles north of Bar Harbor. Another section of the park lies on the Schoodic Peninsula, southeast of Ellsworth, a 1½-hour drive from Bar Harbor. Take U. S. 1 south of Ellsworth, and head east to West Gouldsboro. Go south via Me. 186 to Winter Harbor, then follow signs to the park entrance. The islands—Isle au Haut and Baker Island, can be reached only by boat. Boat schedules are available from the Visitor Center or directly from the boat operators. Airports: Bangor and Bar Harbor.

WHEN TO GO
Acadia is an all-year park, but the main Visitor Center is open from mid-April to October 31. You can expect occasional heavy traffic jams in July and August. Early September is pleasant and less busy. Spectacular fall foliage attracts more crowds around the end of September. Snow and ice close most of the park roads from December through April, but parts of the park are open for cross-country skiing.

GETTING AROUND
Acadia offers a wealth of possibilities for bikers, hikers, horseback/carriage riders, and cross-country skiers—57 miles of carriage roads and 120 miles of hiking trails. Those who don't want

Bass Harbor Head Light has lit the way to Blue Hill Bay since 1858.

MICHAEL MELFORD

to get out of their cars can enjoy the 20-mile Park Loop Road. The Park Service sponsors guided boat trips around the area.

WHAT TO DO
Tour boats are commercially operated, so expect a fee. There are many choices, but the trips sponsored by the NPS have a ranger on board to interpret sights. It is important to make reservations, handled directly with the boat operators.

The **Baker Island** cruise, a half-day trip that leaves from Northeast Harbor, highlights natural as well as human history. Passengers may catch glimpses of ospreys, seals, eider ducks, loons, guillemots, and other seabirds. On the island, sightseers learn about the pioneer life of the Gilley family in the early 19th century and visit the cemetery and lighthouse.

Canoeing is popular on park lakes, especially **Echo Lake** and **Long Pond**. Slightly more adventurous is sea kayaking in the protected areas of Frenchman Bay.

Bicycling is a major attraction for families with children, and no one should visit the park without walking at least one or a few of the trails or carriage roads. These can range from a little stroll through the **Wild Gardens of Acadia** at Sieur de Monts Spring to the park's most difficult challenge, the **Precipice Trail** up Champlain Mountain. The latter should be attempted only by those in good physical condition, with sturdy footwear, and in good weather. The **Acadia Mountain Trail** offers a great view of Somes Sound. Local people who like to get away from crowds recommend the interconnecting trails around Penobscot, Sargent, and Parkman mountains, west of Jordan Pond.

SIDE TRIPS
Whale-watching boats from Bar Harbor and Northeast Harbor are very popular. Some 20 species of whales and porpoises have been spotted during the spring and summer. Birders take these trips to see puffins, storm-petrels, shearwaters, and other oceanic species. Often the boat operators are expert at pointing out seabirds.

Mammoth Cave

The sun beat down from a cloudless sky, and at eight o'clock the temperature strained toward 80°F. A blast of cold air suddenly banished the warmth of the August morning. Staring at an immense black hole in the hillside, people began donning jackets and sweaters. My family and I joined them. We had come, as they had, to tour Mammoth Cave National Park in the hills of south-central Kentucky, and we were about to descend into the longest known cave in the world.

Mammoth contains 350 miles of passages, and researchers map more of the

Squirming through crawlways and crevices lit only by their headlamps,

National Park

by Toni Eugene • Photographed by Chip Clark

system each year. Like thousands of other families my husband, Ned, eight-year-old Ted, six-year-old Elizabeth, and I were visiting for the weekend.

The park, established in 1941, attracts more than 5,000 people a day during the summer months. Most hope to tour the labyrinth of limestone

passages that underlies the 52,830-acre park.

The gaping hole that vented cold air was the Historic Entrance, largest natural opening to Mammoth and, until 1921, the only public entrance. Legend explains that an early settler discovered the cave when he chased a bear through

sightseers on the Wild Cave Tour explore five rugged miles of Mammoth.

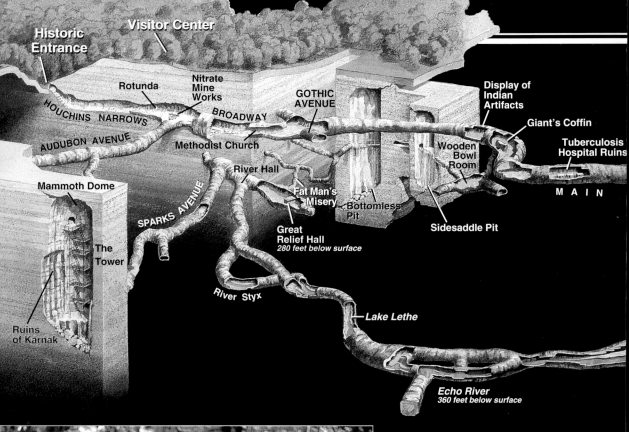

Historic Entrance
Visitor Center
Nitrate Mine Works
Rotunda
GOTHIC AVENUE
Display of Indian Artifacts
HOUCHINS NARROWS
BROADWAY
Giant's Coffin
AUDUBON AVENUE
Methodist Church
Tuberculosis Hospital Ruins
River Hall
Wooden Bowl Room
Mammoth Dome
SPARKS AVENUE
Fat Man's Misery
Bottomless Pit
M A I N
The Tower
Great Relief Hall
280 feet below surface
Sidesaddle Pit
Ruins of Karnak
River Styx
Lake Lethe
Echo River
360 feet below surface

At the Historic Entrance, which led explorers into the cave, rangers prepare visitors for a trip underground.

this hole in the late 1790s. Now concrete stairs lead down; a waterfall cascades off nearby mossy rocks.

"Take one last look up at the sun," our guide, Zona Cetera, advised; then she led

us downward into darkness. Passing through twilight near the entrance, we walked a dirt trail into the Rotunda, a room 142 feet long and nearly as wide. Mammoth got its name from the immense passages and canyons carved out of the limestone by underground rivers, Zona explained.

A caprock of sandstone and shale as thick as 50 feet overlies Mammoth, forming its roof. Below that roof, ancient rivers flowed horizontally, working in cracks and between layers of rock to dissolve subsurface limestone and hollow out passageways. The water always flowed downward. There are now five known

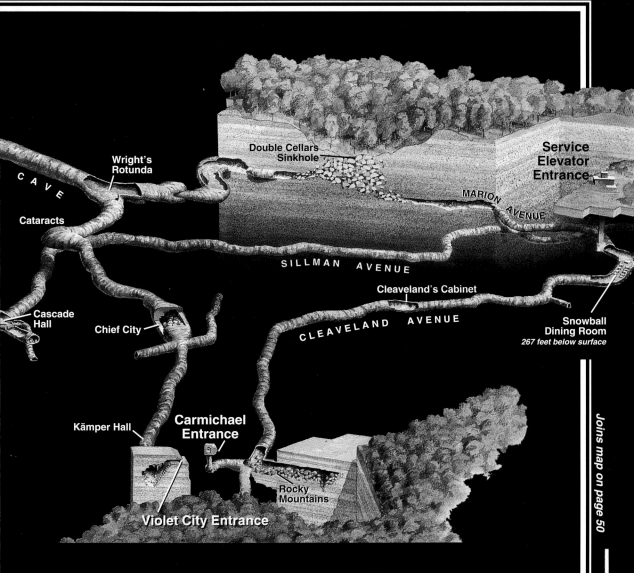

Wright's Rotunda

C A V E

Cataracts

Double Cellars Sinkhole

Service Elevator Entrance

MARION AVENUE

SILLMAN AVENUE

Cascade Hall

Chief City

Cleaveland's Cabinet

CLEAVELAND AVENUE

Snowball Dining Room
267 feet below surface

Kämper Hall

Carmichael Entrance

Rocky Mountains

Violet City Entrance

Joins map on page 50

levels of passageways in Mammoth, each connected to the level above it.

We were exploring in the second level. Discreet lighting and Zona's flashlight revealed the Rotunda's immense curving walls, arched ceilings of brown and gray, man-made vats, and wooden piping. This was the room where, during the War of 1812, 70 slaves equipped with candles or burning rags mined saltpeter to make gunpowder.

The passage narrowed. As the dampness and mustiness increased, Elizabeth hugged her jacket, reminding me that the temperature in Mammoth hovers at around 54°F. Like my family, I clutched damp railings, ducked my head, and descended steep steps. We were approaching, said Zona, the 105-foot-deep Bottomless Pit. It, like the other vertical shafts in Mammoth, was created by ground-

Showcasing some 12 miles of subterranean trails, a cutaway of Mammoth reveals different levels of the 350-mile system.

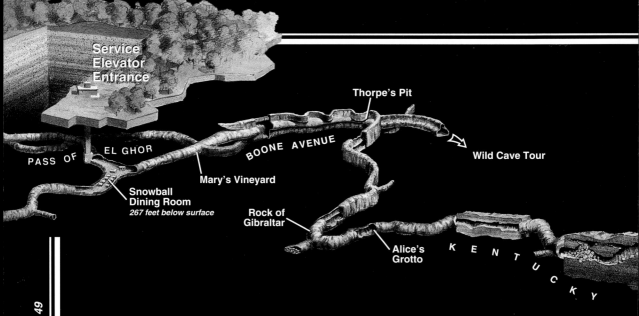

Service Elevator Entrance

Thorpe's Pit

PASS OF EL GHOR

BOONE AVENUE

Wild Cave Tour

Mary's Vineyard

Snowball Dining Room
267 feet below surface

Rock of Gibraltar

Alice's Grotto

K E N T U C K Y

Joins map on page 49

Underground streams carved horizontal passsages in the cave. Vertical seepage at Frozen Niagara created the most colorful flowstone, stalactites, and stalagmites in Mammoth.

water seeping downward through cracks and sinks in the sandstone that caps the cave system. Beyond it Elizabeth and Ted breezed through a winding hundred-foot-long passage called Fat Man's Misery. Ned and I added polish to the thigh-high passage already smoothed by millions who had wiggled past before us. Zona warned us, then turned out the few lights and her flashlight. Silence and darkness settled around us. It was total— absolute—our initiation into the world buried beneath the wooded hills above our heads.

Returning to that world of light, we passed through an enormous shaft called Mammoth Dome. Water dripped from the ceiling 192 feet above us, a reminder that the cave is growing even today.

Clambering up nearly a

hundred steps of a steel tower to reach our starting point, I glanced back. After two hours in the cave, I was strangely reluctant to leave it, unready to face the blazing light and heat that awaited me.

That same reluctance to return to the surface marked two other trips we took into Mammoth. The Lantern Tour, offered in all seasons except winter, re-creates an old-time excursion through unlit parts of the cave. Visitors carry 15-candlepower kerosene lanterns whose flickering glow lights the path. Our guide, Chester Guy, regaled us with stories as he led us through Broadway Avenue to a pair of stone huts. They are, he explained, the remains of a hospital established in 1842 by Dr. John Croghan, who noted

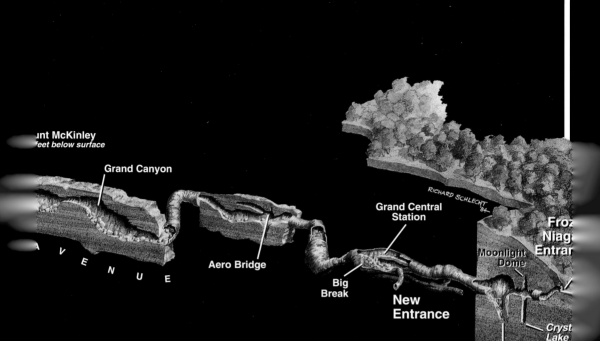

Mount McKinley
...feet below surface

Grand Canyon

A V E N U E

Aero Bridge

Big Break

New Entrance

Grand Central Station

RICHARD SCHLECHT '84

Moonlight Dome

Froz... Niag... Entrar...

Cryst... Lake

Frozen Niagara
130 feet below surface

that nothing decomposed in the unchanging cave environment and thought the consistent climate might benefit tuberculosis patients. Unfortunately, the patients fared poorly, and the experiment was abandoned.

We switchbacked up and down the three-mile-long path for three hours, our line of lanterns bobbing and twisting like a string of fireflies, but I was still unprepared when we surfaced. The midday heat, after the coolness in the cave, fogged my glasses instantly. I stumbled, scrubbed at them, and fought an urge to retreat into the comfortable darkness.

Shorter but no less compelling was a tour called Frozen Niagara. Because the Mammoth system was carved by water flowing horizontally, there are few travertine formations such as stalagmites. Travertine forms when water carrying dissolved limestone flows vertically. The Frozen Niagara focuses on Mammoth's travertine. We passed stalactites, which form as limestone-laden water drips from the ceiling, and stalagmites, created by that water plopping onto the cave floor.

Beyond Crystal Lake, a green pool cupped in rock 60 feet below the trail, we entered a room jammed with pillars, columns, rocky curls, and stony twists. Amid them loomed Frozen Niagara, a 75-foot-tall and 50-foot-wide cascade of orange-white flowstone, which forms as water flows over ledges.

Ted grabbed my arm as we shuffled through the gloom. "Look," he crowed, pointing to a crevice near the trail, "bats!"

As we passed, they fidgeted and darted away. They were eastern pipistrels—one of twelve bat species, two of them endangered, known to use the cave. More than 700 species of animals have been discovered in the park.

Some, such as bats and the blonde crickets with long

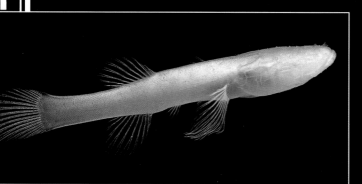

antennae we saw near the cave entrances, are trogloxenes, which make nightly food forays to the surface, then return to the cave. Others, such as cave shrimp and crayfish, are troglobites—animals that have adapted exclusively to life in total darkness. The importance and fragility of the cave's ecosystem helped earn Mammoth designation by UNESCO as a World Heritage Site in 1981 and as an International Biosphere Reserve in 1990.

Although the pull of the cave and its creatures is powerful, much of Mammoth's magic, like much of the park, lies above ground.

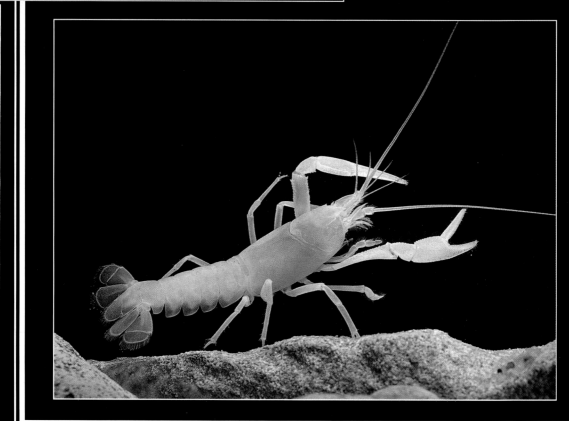

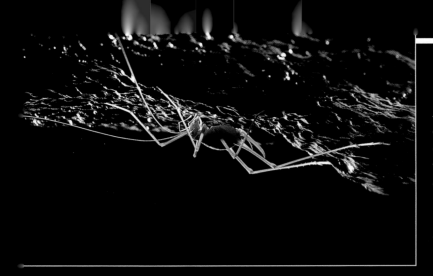

All legs and antennae, a cave cricket maneuvers easily along the ceiling in Mammoth. The crickets surface at night to feed. Troglobites, such as blindfish, spend their entire lives below ground. Like blind crayfish, they have developed sensory organs to feel their way in the dark. Twelve species of troglobites in Mammoth exist

More than 60 miles of trails lace the 82½-square-mile park, meandering through second-growth woodlands of sycamore, hickory, oak, and hemlock. Hikes usually range from half-mile strolls to six-hour struggles. As Ned and I ambled toward the Green River on the Echo River Trail one afternoon, Ted and Elizabeth raced ahead. Chipmunks and squirrels scolded the speeding children, but they slowed almost immediately to watch a white-tailed deer and her fawn prance through sunlight and shadows.

We paused at Mammoth Dome Sink, where pawpaw trees arch above a dark sinkhole laced with ferns. Here groundwater funnels into the cave through a hidden crack in the caprock. At a leafy dell farther along the trail, water seeps out of the cave at Echo Springs and flows onward to feed the Green River.

The river slices east to west through the park. When it floods, it pumps nutrient-rich rainwater into the cave—fresh food for many cave species. Cruising the greenish-brown waters on the *Miss Green River II* ferry, we watched a blue heron lift off from a log, studied three deer as they moseyed through stands of sycamore and birch, and admired sunlight dancing on boughs of silver maple.

Thick black clouds had gathered by late afternoon, when we hiked back to our hotel. Squirrels chattered wildly, and a deer raced by. We picked up our pace. "Faster, " Ned urged the kids, "we'll get wet." We did that. Lightning split the sky, followed immediately by a boom of thunder. Elizabeth shrieked, and we started running. Though drenched and shivering by the time we reached our rooms, we were laughing, too. We agreed that the world of light in Mammoth is every bit as exciting as the world of darkness.

One of the goals of the park, then Superintendent

Dave Mihalic told me the next morning, is to show visitors both worlds of Mammoth. He credits his staff with creating tours that appeal to many different types of visitors—from the wheelchair-accessible boardwalk of the Heritage Trail to the kids-only Trog Tour.

The latter offers a short nature walk above ground and a journey into cave passageways not seen on other tours. Families visit Mammoth, he told me, and the park strives to present programs that each member, from child to grandparent, can enjoy.

The park is obviously succeeding. By 9:30 Monday morning every tour was sold out. When I left Dave's office opposite the Visitor Center the scene was one of controlled chaos. A people parade cruised by—fat ones, skinny ones, senior citizens, and toddlers. A loudspeaker announced upcoming tours; bulletin boards advertised slide shows in the auditorium and evening activities. The parking lot reflected the human variety, housing Harleys and Hondas, campers and Cadillacs that sported license plates from Maine to California.

We zigzagged through the tide of visitors to reach our car, and again I felt that reluctance to leave. I envied the milling hundreds their first blast of cold air—a breeze that would awaken them to the many wonders of Mammoth Cave.

Flowstone drapes the emerald depths of Crystal Lake 60 feet below the trail near the Frozen Niagara entrance. Submerged lights illuminate the clarity of the 12-foot-deep pool.

Visiting Mammoth Cave

KENTUCKY
ESTABLISHED: July 1, 1941
SIZE: 52,830 acres
HEADQUARTERS
Mammoth Cave, Kentucky 42259
Phone (502) 758-2328

HOW TO GET THERE
The park is 9 miles northwest of Interstate 65, about 85 miles south of Louisville and north of Nashville, Tenn. From the south, take Exit 48 at Park City and head northwest on Ky. 255 to the park; from the north, take Exit 53 at Cave City and head northwest on Ky. 70 to the park. Nearest airports: Nashville and Louisville.

WHEN TO GO
All-year park. Underground, all days are about the same. Frequent tours are offered in the summer, when crowds are larger. Fewer tours are offered the rest of the year, but they are easier to get into. Weekend tours are more difficult to get tickets for all year. It is recommended that you call the park before you go to reserve tickets for specific tours. Unfortunately, many people come to the park, especially during peak season, and find all the tours are sold out. Tour schedules change throughout the year.

Great Smoky Mountains & Shenandoah National Parks

by Scott Thybony • Photographed by Jay Dickman

Steep ridges crest above a sea of clouds in the Great Smoky Mountains. The range takes its name from the mist produced by leaves transpiring water and hydrocarbons.

Patches of mist stir as a deer steps softly from the cover of the woods, ears alert. Another appears and another, drifting into the open fields of Cades Cove, a pocket of the Great Smoky Mountains. I sit on a knoll, watching them graze and listening for a sound I've never heard.

"Stay until dark," Lois Caughron told me earlier in the day, "and you might hear a wolf. They were out there howling the past two nights." A dim light far across the cove marks the house where she and her husband, Kermit, live. They are the last residents of a mountain community that moved away when the Great Smokies became a national park. As dusk thickens in the hollows vacated by the mountain people, I wait for the red wolves to return.

In the 1930s two national parks took root in the southern Appalachian Mountains: Great Smoky Mountains National Park, straddling the border of Tennessee and North Carolina, and Shenandoah National Park, stretching along the crest of the Blue Ridge Mountains in Virginia. The Blue Ridge Parkway links the Appalachian parks with 469 winding miles of scenic highway.

Unlike western parks, which were set aside before major settlement occurred, these eastern highlands were home to families who had cleared and farmed much of the land for generations. Before the park was created, loggers had cut 70 to 80 percent of the old-growth forest in the Great Smokies. Almost no virgin timber remained in the Blue Ridge parklands—and no wolves in either park.

Much of the eastern wildlands disappeared before they could be protected. But were they gone forever? I've come to the southern Appalachians to look for signs of renewal half a century after the creation of the national parks. My travels will take me into regions of the Smokies and Blue Ridge once heavily logged and into the tall, old-growth forest. Along the way I will talk with people who have witnessed in their lifetimes the return of a wilder country.

Earlier in the day Chris Lucash entered his office behind the Cades Cove ranger station. A field biologist with the U. S. Fish and Wildlife Service, Lucash heads the team reintroducing red wolves to the park. "It's been a long night," he said.

A telemetry receiver for tracking wolves lay on his desk. All the released animals wear radio collars to make continuous monitoring possible. Lucash said he had spent most of the night chasing a wolf that had strayed beyond the park. "Sometimes," he said with a slight smile, "they have trouble reading the park boundary signs."

Great Smoky Mountains is the first national park to reintroduce these large predators. At the time of my visit ten free-ranging wolves lived in the park, six in Cades Cove. That spring, Lucash said, the park's first wolf pups were born in the wild.

To find the wolves, I first had to lose myself in bumper-to-bumper traffic. More than nine million visitors enter the Great

Smokies each year—more than any other national park—and most of them see it from their cars. Leaving the biologist's office, I joined a line of campers and cars looping slowly through Cades Cove, population 2. After a few miles I turned down an unpaved lane leading to the Caughrons' home. To preserve the cove's historic setting, park managers needed a farmer and his cattle to keep the land open, free of trees. They allowed the Caughrons to stay—the last of 6,600 landowners who once inhabited the Great Smokies.

Passing beehives and a patch of corn, I pulled up to a house with no electric lines feeding into it. Lois Caughron walked to the gate to talk, wearing a print dress. Her husband, Kermit, in his 80s, was away cutting hay with his sons. Lois told me the wolves had been coming close the last few nights. She paused and looked across the field toward the slow-moving traffic on the road. "People ask me if we watch the wild animals," she said. "'No,' I tell them, 'we watch the tourists.'"

That evening I sit waiting for the red wolves as the mountains fade in the gathering darkness. Clouds push up the steep slopes and sink back as if the air has taken on weight and mass. Two hours pass before I hear something across the field—a bark or a yip, I'm not sure. It happens again, and then a single note begins, low and mournful. Rising in pitch, it builds into a full howl. The wolves are gathering in a small grove across the meadow. Another wolf joins in and another until a sustained, wavering chorus fills the night. Each haunting cry rises out of a remote, wilder past.

I finally pull myself away and return to the road. A truck coasts up with the lights off. "Are you listening to them?" a woman asks with a hill country twang, her eyes shining. "It's a beautiful sound."

Next day, a chorus of human voices joins together, drawing out a note for all it's worth. A group of local musicians is playing a fast-lick rendition of a traditional mountain song. They've gathered for Old Timers' Day with thousands of other music lovers at the Cable Mill, a few miles from where the wolves were howling last night.

Rain has forced the pickers to squeeze onto the porch of a pioneer home, concerned more about their instruments staying dry than about getting wet themselves. Dozens of other musicians crowd under every roof or tree that gives some shelter.

Caught up in the music, one old-timer can't keep his feet from moving. He clogs away as the rain comes down, dressed in bib overalls with a fedora on his head. Someone in the band gives a holler, and he answers with a loud whoop. A man watching from under the eaves of a shed comments rather dryly, "That rain'll learn him."

When the piece ends, a farmer displaced from the mountains in the 1930s asks me a question. "I often wondered," he begins

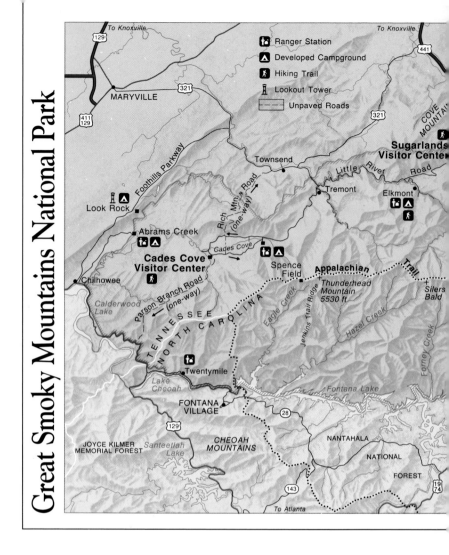

politely, "does this music sound as different to you as rock and roll does to me? That rock and roll doesn't make sense to me."

His music, drawn from these hills, spans the generations. Nearby, a grandmother picks a guitar next to a young girl missing her front teeth, who saws away on a fiddle. The gray-haired woman sings about raven black hair and a wildwood flower.

Hearing more music coming from the barn, I wander over and meet two sisters, Edith Gregory and Hester Wilburn, who grew up in Cades Cove. "I broke my back many a time throwing corn in that corncrib out there," Edith says, nodding toward a wooden shed moved here by the Park Service from her father's place.

Edith was 20 and Hester 15 when their family had to relocate in the 1930s. "It was bad having to leave," Edith says, recalling the day she rode away from home for the last time. "I was mad. I just wished those mountains would clap together so no one could go there again. I shouldn't have thought that, but that's how I felt. How would you feel if somebody took away your home?" When I ask if they would return, given the chance, they both answer no, and

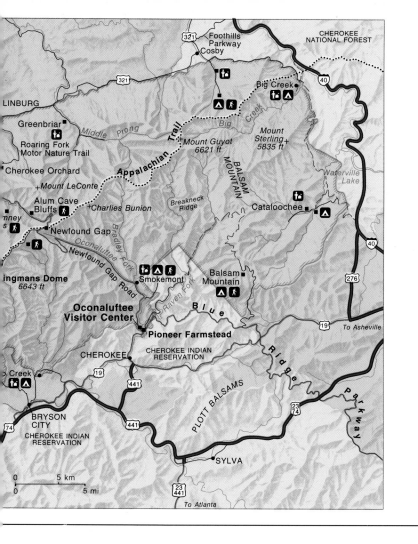

Established in 1934, Great Smoky Mountains National Park contains 800 square miles of rare natural beauty on the border of Tennessee and North Carolina. The mountain sanctuary draws more than nine million visitors a year, a greater number than any other national park. But those willing to leave the car behind can still find solitude on the park's 800 miles of footpaths.

then laugh at their quick reply. "Not without electricity," Edith says.

Having left Cades Cove for more remote country, I begin a trip across the Smokies on the first day of fall. Scott Danals, a local white-water canoeist, and I paddle across Fontana Lake on the North Carolina side of the park. He steers the canoe toward the far shore where the Great Smokies tumble downward in steep, tree-thick slopes. We glide across the lake under a sky as clear and sharp as the new season. A woodworker by trade, Danals has crafted our paddles from five different kinds of native trees—light and strong with just the right cant to the blade for flat-water travel.

As we near the foot of the mountains, the wall of solid green before us breaks into a mosaic of individual trees, many unfamiliar to me. Botanists have identified 130 species of trees in the park and more than 1,500 species of flowering plants. We round a densely wooded headland and turn up an inlet leading to Hazel Creek. Danals eases the canoe between shallow boulders, landing where the creek riffles into the lake. A few cicadas buzz in the highest branches as we start up a road shown as a trail on the park map. The lake and high mountains have isolated this region, so I am somewhat surprised to find a road in good repair. At certain times of the year, Danals explains, the Park Service takes local families back to pay their respects at cemeteries they were forced to leave behind.

As we hike up the road, my companion tells me he once ran a canoe down Hazel Creek at high-water stage. To reach the headwaters, he trekked 11 miles from Clingmans Dome—at 6,643 feet the highest mountain in the park but the nearest route to the creek. Danals carried a 40-pound canoe on his shoulders, causing some confusion among the first hikers he met. "Are you on the right trail?" they wanted to know. The next party, even more puzzled, asked, "Are we on the right trail?"

A few miles above the lake, Danals and I veer off onto an overgrown path. Ruined walls soon appear in the woods before us, green with moss and vine and overshadowed by tall trees. Here a sawmill processed as much as 100,000 board feet of lumber a day before it was abandoned. Roots now twist into mounds of tumbled masonry, covered by leaf mold, liverwort, and lichen. The forest is slowly absorbing the mill, wall by wall and brick by brick.

Even less remains of Proctor, the busy lumber town of a thousand residents that supported the mill. The lumber company closed operations in 1928, and the remaining inhabitants left a few years later when the land became a national park.

Danals turns back to the lake, and I head up the road through a tunnel of overarching trees. Sunlight hits the canopy above, turning the topmost leaves a luminous green. Only fragments of light run the gauntlet of branch and leaf and penetrate clear to the forest floor. Segments of a railroad bed, vague and overgrown, parallel the road for a stretch, only to fade out like an old memory.

The valley narrows and the creek picks up speed, funneling through a natural spillway worn in the bedrock. Next to it grow giant-leafed magnolia trees and tall sycamores. I continue walking, passing through a dark hollow filled with eastern hemlocks.

By late afternoon I reach my designated campsite. After pitching a tent near the creek, I find an old road winding up a ridge above Bone Valley. The name came from a profusion of bones found here after a blizzard in the 1880s trapped a herd of cattle.

I follow the road to see where it goes. Fallen needles and leaves form a soft, matted surface underfoot. A boulder by the road has turned green and spongy beneath a growth of moss and fungus inches thick. Next to it grow a few mushrooms—one red, a couple of white ones, and the smallest a vivid blue.

The road narrows to a trail before topping the ridge and entering a clearing filled with graves. Rough native stones, planted at the head and foot, mark most of the 80 gravesites, and bronze plaques identify a half dozen Confederate veterans.

At the outbreak of the Civil War, recruiters entered Hazel Creek to the beat of a drum. Everyone gathered to hear the stirring speeches and watch the novelty of a Punch-and-Judy puppet show. Caught up in the excitement, several young men enlisted and marched off to war. Of the first three volunteers, only one returned home alive.

After dark I meet a party of North Carolina fishermen camped nearby. They sit around a low campfire dressed in dark camouflage, cooking the day's catch. When it's ready, their leader hands me a plate with a pan-fried rainbow trout and fried cornmeal dough. The hush puppy is a reminder that this is the *southern* Appalachians.

A faint light filters through the forest early the next morning as I break camp and walk down Hazel Creek. I turn up Sugar Fork where the road branches and continue another mile or two, studying the map. Tangled rhododendrons screen the mouth of Little Fork where I leave the roadway to look for the ghost of a primeval forest.

Last of the mountain people allowed to stay on after the Great Smokies became a national park, Lois and Kermit Caughron help the Park Service maintain Cades Cove.

In 1904 a librarian named Horace Kephart headed alone into the most remote corner of this mountain wilderness. At the age of 42, he had found his career in ruins, his marriage a shambles, his health broken. He left St. Louis and ended up in the Great Smokies, living in a log cabin on Little Fork.

"He was searching for a place to begin again," said George Ellison, who researched Kephart's life and career. "He didn't come to the mountains for a cure but to find a sense of himself. It was his way of getting back on track. And it worked." Ellison, a naturalist and writer, sat in his Bryson City office. On the wall hung an old photograph of Kephart resting on the crest of the Smokies, staring into the far distance. Kephart became an expert in wilderness living and a widely read outdoor writer. But his most important work was *Our Southern Highlanders*, a story of (Continued on page 82)

FOLLOWING PAGES: Autumn paints the ridges above Cades Cove—first the highest crests, where the weather is cooler, then moving lower each day.

*Reintroduced into
the wild, endangered
red wolves skirt the
edge of Cades Cove
(opposite).*

*Radio collars on the
wolves enable biologist
Chris Lucash to track
their movements
electronically as
Barron Crawford scans
the forest openings.*

JAMES VALENTINE (ABOVE); JOHN NETHERTON (BELOW AND OPPOSITE)

Fog settles in the treetops above a tangle of moss-covered logs. Damp and shaded, the forest provides an ideal habitat for an amazing variety of amphibians. A tree frog (right) rests

on a leaf, while a
cave salamander (left),
one of 27 species
of salamanders found
in the Smokies, pauses
on a clump of moss.

White-tailed deer,
once scarce in the
mountains, thrive
under the protection
of the park. Herds
graze the open fields of
Cades Cove and
Cataloochee during
much of the day.
Many visitors travel
to the Smokies for a
chance to see the park's
abundant wildlife.

JOHN NETHERTON

Perched on a tree limb, a black bear checks its surroundings (opposite). Agile climbers, black bears often den in tree hollows high above the ground. Alert to danger, a mother black bear (left) stays close to her young. A vehicle slows as cubs dash across the road (above). Such bear sightings may bring traffic to a halt, causing it to back up in "bear jams."

73

Flowers burst from a thick tangle of rhododendrons high in the Great Smoky Mountains (opposite). Each spring, wildflower enthusiasts converge on the park to witness the vivid displays of its 1,500 species of flowering plants, such as the wild bleeding heart (above). Petals of the crested dwarf iris (left) open in symmetrical patterns.

FOLLOWING PAGES: *Hikers Rhonda Howard and Alan Gentry pause in the warm light of late autumn on a peak called Charlies Bunion.*

Maple leaves add
another layer of color
to moss-covered rocks
on the Roaring Fork
(below). Leaves
blanket the Heintooga
Round Bottom Road,
where the Danals
family bicycles through
the fall woods.

TIM BLACK

Frosted spires rise like ghosts along the highest crest of the Smokies (opposite). Nearby, the Dziezic family strolls along the Appalachian Trail through a spruce-fir forest encased in ice. The famous pathway winds for 2,000 miles from Georgia to Maine.

the mountain people whose way of life he shared. "It's the classic study of southern Appalachia," Ellison said.

Avoiding the undergrowth along the bed of the hollow, I follow the trace of an old road. It soon disappears into a patch of rhododendrons, forcing me to take a wandering course up the creek. Vines as thick as a wrist loop down from tall trees. I detour around deadfall, branch, and brier so interwoven they appear to be a single organism.

The forest light fades to a smoky green, absorbed by the tree cover and gathering clouds. Logs overgrown with moss jam the creek bed ahead under the low-hanging boughs of hemlock. The dark branches appear to hold the night long into morning. I continue higher up the creek to where the hollow widens.

Kephart left Little Fork after a stay of three years. When he returned a few years later, the lumbermen had come and gone. He found stumps and slash piles where ancient trees once met overhead "like cathedral roofs."

"My log cabin…has fallen in ruin," he wrote. "The great forest wherein it nestled is falling, too, before the loggers' steel." Kephart felt the Smokies had saved his life and worked to repay the debt by promoting the national park.

Little remains to mark his cabin site. A level spot next to the creek shows where a dwelling might have stood. Around it, un-branched trunks of maple, oak, and tulip tree grow skyward, tall and straight. Beneath them, a few scattered stumps have resisted decay. I rest next to an old chestnut stump. A sapling, no thicker than a pen-cil, spindles up from the rotted core of a tree that once grew three feet across. The forest is returning to Little Fork—not Kephart's primeval world, but a new forest with its own dynamic beauty.

Retracing my steps, I continue up Sugar Fork to Jenkins Ridge Trail and begin the long ascent to the top of the Smokies. A mile up the trail, the scene explodes in a whirl of startled wings as a grouse flies downslope, dodging trees as it tucks close to the ground.

Soon after resuming a steady gait, I'm surprised by a large ani-mal suddenly crashing into the undergrowth ahead. Branches snap loudly under its full weight as I catch a glimpse of a bear, black as a shadow. It escapes deep into a thicket and stops. I can't see it, but it must be listening and sniffing, trying to read my intentions—which are to put some distance between us.

The black bear has been feeding on wild cherries. During fall, it can gain three to five pounds a day, gorging on nuts and berries be-fore finding a hollow tree and curling up for the winter. Bears don't hibernate as some other animals such as ground squirrels do, but fall into a state known to biologists as "carnivore lethargy."

Light rain begins falling in midafternoon. I can hear it hitting the canopy long before the first raindrops reach the ground. It stops, but the forest continues to drip long after the storm has passed. I hear each raindrop falling from leaf to leaf as it ricochets downward.

High on the ridge, the trail tunnels through thick clumps of rhododendrons before entering a grassy clearing studded with ser-viceberry trees. The sky opens in all directions. After being buried in green for two days, I can see again. Ranges toss up one after another, rippling away to the horizon in a succession of ridges. I've crested the Smokies, topping out at Spence Field, 4,958 feet in elevation.

As I stand looking below, I hear voices for the first time all day. Backpackers are coming along the Appalachian Trail, a 2,000-mile, Maine-to-Georgia footpath that crosses almost 70 miles of the park. Two hikers appear, carrying hefty packs. The Atlanta businessmen are spending a few days covering a segment of the "AT" they haven't walked before. "For me it's therapy," says Bob Andrew. His friend Kerry Myers agrees.

In the spring the two men sometimes go to the start of the Appalachian Trail at Springer Mountain, Georgia. They try to guess which of the through-hikers will complete the five-million-step, four-month trek to Maine. "We scratched one guy off the list right

Snow blankets a pioneer cabin maintained by the Park Service as a reminder of the mountain people who settled in Cades Cove long ago. Log walls chinked with mud once sheltered the John Oliver family from winter storms. Settlers poured into the cove soon after the Cherokee Indians ceded the land to Tennessee in 1819.

away," Bob says. "He showed up at the trailhead carrying a suitcase."

The three of us continue to the trail shelter where we unpack our gear for the night. Heavy wire mesh encloses the open front of the stone lean-to. Tossing my sleeping bag on the top bunk, I feel as though I've checked into a zoo where they keep the humans in cages and let the wildlife roam free.

As evening approaches, I return to the open ridgetop. Mist streams through the treetops next to me, shredded by the branches. The air has grown visibly fluid with clouds climbing out of the coves below. They rise in Tennessee, following the wind as they flow across the mountain crest and tumble into North Carolina.

After hiking down to Cades Cove the next morning, I drive to the Eastern Cherokee country that borders the park in North Carolina. In 1838 the mountain Cherokee hid in the wildest pockets of the Smokies to keep from being captured. Soldiers rounded up about 17,000 Cherokees and forced them at bayonet point to migrate westward. But hundreds of the tribe who took refuge in the mountains remained free. Their descendants now form the Eastern Cherokee band.

Water nourishes a wild strawberry bush in the green world of the Great Smokies. Each year more than 85 inches of precipitation fall on the mountains in the form of rain and snow.

JOHN NETHERTON

"*Joog-su-sdee*," Myrtle Johnson says, pronouncing the Cherokee word carefully. "That's what we call the mountains. The word means, 'It smokes.'" Former tribal council member, Myrtle Johnson lives in the traditional community of Big Cove on the Raven Fork of the Oconaluftee River. "We call it the Raven Rock Fork," Myrtle says. The name refers to a prominent outcrop above Big Cove. "Ravens gather at that rock. And the Raven Mockers. They're the most feared shamans. They used to imitate ravens, calling like them. They used to fly to the rock."

Some Cherokee, Myrtle says, still use traditional methods of healing. Once when she was sick, she remembered the elders had said to drink springwater that flows from the east. She searched until she found a branch flowing the proper direction and drank enough to cure herself. "Water," she says, "is the best medicine."

By midafternoon I'm descending Breakneck Ridge in a rugged corner of the park missed by the loggers. Somewhere below runs the Raven Fork, hidden in a dense stand of old-growth timber. The national park contains about 100,000 acres of old growth—90 percent of the virgin forest remaining in the eastern United States.

A trace of an abandoned trail, called a manway, fades in and out of sight as it winds through the undergrowth, dividing into a maze of faint possibilities. A brier patch forces me to back off and hunt a way around it. I pass ragged stumps higher than I can reach and enter a grove of immense trees rising straight and solemn.

What's believed to be the nation's largest red spruce, 123 feet tall with a girth of more than 14 feet, grows here on Breakneck Ridge. I throw myself off balance by craning my head back far enough to see the top of one tree. So many big trees grow on this steep slope, I can't be sure which holds the record.

The pathway drops beneath a massive root, covered with moss as soft and green as baize. The air hangs saturated; water trickles underfoot; leaves drip. Ahead, two trees with interlocked roots have fallen into a rhododendron thicket, blocking the way with a knot of branches and brush.

The downed trees have left a hole in the forest canopy. I look across to a facing ridge, but all I see is more green—Glenn Cardwell's wall of green. The park naturalist was born in the Smokies before the founding of the park. He has seen the forest reclaim the once settled mountains. "I have the same views my ancestors had when they arrived in the Smokies in 1805," he said. "I can look out and see the same wall of green."

As I search for a way past the deadfall, a foot slips and I slide into the brush, swallowed by the green tangle. I crawl back a foot or two and pull myself over the fallen trees. Pushing on, I bushwhack through another thicket a few hundred feet away. Some country is geologically rough; this is biologically rough.

Mist begins to fill the spaces among the trees, shifting with each breath of air. I feel a twinge of warning. If a fog sets in, I'll be unable to find my way back to camp.

Turning around, I slog upslope with my boots soaked and my clothes hanging wet and muddy. In places I pull myself up with branch and root. Emerging out of the mist, I reach the half-light of the ridgetop forest. I return to camp and slump down on the nearest log, too tired to brush off a red maple leaf that lands on my shoulder. I sit and wonder if the leaves have started falling in the Shenandoah country to the north.

Two ravens hang suspended in the wind above Old Rag Mountain, several hundred miles north of the Great Smokies. Outstretched wings rock back and forth, balancing against the rush of air. Suddenly one bird dips a wing and turns, letting the wind sling it into the void, 2,000 feet above the ground.

Old Rag, detached from the central portion of the Blue Ridge range to the west, stands on the boundary of Shenandoah National Park. Forested ridges rise on the wild side of the mountain, and pasturelands roll away in the distance on the tame. Bare granite, a billion years old, pokes through the tree cover on the summit.

Taking shelter on a ledge out of the wind, I look across at the main range that stretches north and south, buttressed by numerous

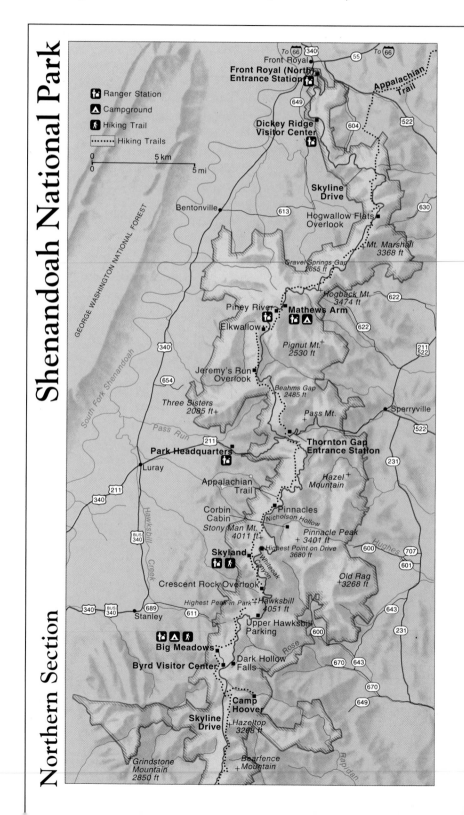

Ranger Station
Campground
Hiking Trail
Hiking Trails

0 — 5 km
0 — 5 mi

To 66 340
Front Royal
To 66
55
Front Royal (North)
Entrance Station
Appalachian Trail
649
Dickey Ridge
Visitor Center
604
522
Skyline
Drive
630
Bentonville
613
Hogwallow Flats
Overlook
Mt. Marshall
3368 ft
Gravel Springs Gap
2655 ft
Hogback Mt.
3474 ft
622
Piney River
Mathews Arm
622
Elkwallow
Pignut Mt.
2530 ft
211
522
Jeremy's Run
Overlook
Beahms Gap
2485 ft
Three Sisters
2085 ft+
Pass Mt.
Sperryville
Pass Run
522
Thornton Gap
Entrance Station
Park Headquarters
211
Luray
231
Hazel
Mountain
Appalachian
Trail
Corbin
Cabin
Pinnacles
Nicholson Hollow
Stony Man Mt.
4011 ft
Pinnacle Peak
3401 ft
600
707
Highest Point on Drive
3680 ft
601
Skyland
Old Rag
3268 ft
Crescent Rock Overlook
Highest Peak in Park
Hawksbill
4051 ft
643
340
689
611
Upper Hawksbill
Parking
600
231
Stanley
Big Meadows
Byrd Visitor Center
Dark Hollow
Falls
670
643
670
Camp
Hoover
649
Skyline
Drive
Hazeltop
3268 ft
Grindstone
Mountain
2850 ft
Bearfence
Mountain
Rapidan

GEORGE WASHINGTON NATIONAL FOREST

South Fork Shenandoah

Hawksbill Creek

Whiteoak Canyon

Hughes

Rose

spur ridges. The air is cider sharp and so transparent the distance has an edge to it. Splashes of yellow, red, and brown brighten the green expanse. Cloud shadows, as black as ravens, fly down the slopes of Hawksbill Mountain, a hunched shoulder against the skyline. Its

Shenandoah National Park, established in 1935, covers the forested slopes of Virginia's Blue Ridge Mountains. Each year some two million visitors come for the wide vistas along the 105-mile Skyline Drive, the autumn foliage, and a 500-mile network of footpaths. Inhabited by Indians and settlers for hundreds of years before becoming a park, the mountains have returned to a wilder state. Forests with more than 100 species of trees now cover 95 percent of the park.

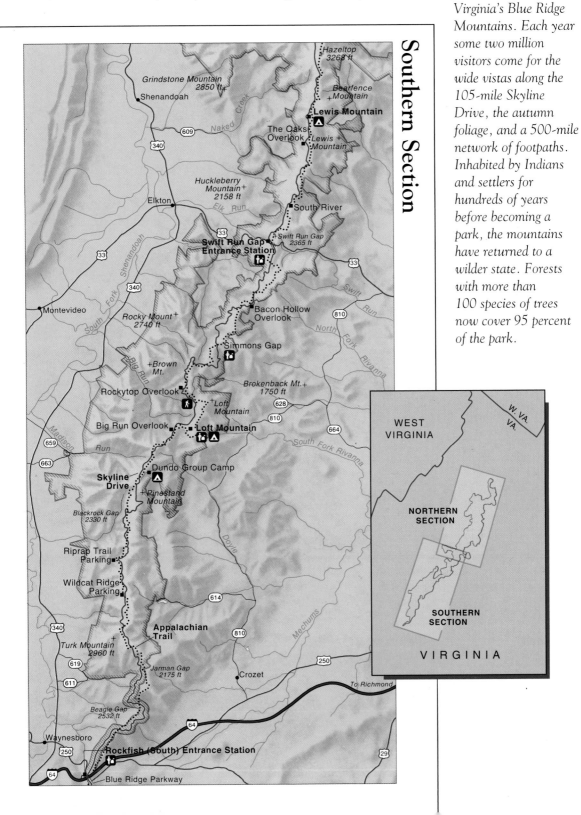

Southern Section

elevation of 4,051 feet makes it the highest point in the park. No other hiker has come in sight, even though it's a fall weekend on one of the park's most popular trails.

As soon as I turn back, voices float up from below. A father has let his young son take the lead. The boy strides up the trail searching for swatches of blue paint that mark the route across the boulder outcrops. Other parties weave up the ridge behind them—families, friends, students. The file of hikers climbing the trail doesn't let up. Everyone I pass is smiling.

"I have traveled around the world," says Bob Hiedemann, pausing to catch his breath. The art dealer leans on a tapered walking stick. "There's no place as beautiful. There's a human dimension to the Blue Ridge that's just right."

The pathway turns into a billy goat trail where hikers take turns scrambling up a fissure in the cliff rock. I wait at the top for a chance to descend. So many hands have grabbed the tree branch next to me, the grain of the wood is as smooth as polished furniture.

The Appalachian parks are islands of wild country in a region long settled and heavily populated. Each year some two million people visit Shenandoah National Park. Park rangers estimate that 20 to 30 million people can reach the park on a tank of gas. But those who seek solitude can still find it.

Next day, I walk with Darwin and Eileen Lambert, naturalists and writers, above their home on the west side of the Blue Ridge. The woods lie still and quiet, giving the feeling we have the place to ourselves. "At the peak of the leaf season," says Eileen, "we can walk out back into the park and never see anyone for the whole day."

Wearing a flannel shirt, with binoculars strapped around her neck, she leans over to inspect a yellow jacket nest dug up by a bear. Darwin, wearing a felt hat and a full gray mustache, points his walking stick toward a hollow hammering coming from deeper in the forest. "Pileated woodpecker," he says with a smile as he recognizes an old friend.

I avoid stepping on a mushroom growing in the trail, as Eileen gives its scientific name. For breakfast that morning she served morel mushrooms, locally called "merkels," that she had gathered last spring. Eileen and her husband live at the foot of the mountains in a two-story log cabin built in the 1850s. Darwin appraises a black locust snag next to the trail—the wood he prefers to heat his home. The locust is a pioneer species, he says. Most are now dead or dying, overshadowed by other trees in the natural forest succession.

The Blue Ridge looked different when Darwin first arrived in 1935, bicycling out from Washington, D. C. A year later he was sworn in as the first employee of the new Shenandoah National

Park. "I had to get away from that crowded city," he says, eyes twinkling. "I couldn't stand it any more."

Pastures at that time spread along the ridgetops, and cleared fields ran along the creeks. Perhaps a third of the park lay open, stripped of timber. First the locust, persimmon, and Virginia pine appeared, Darwin says, followed by chestnut oak, red oak, white pine, and others of the hundred species of trees found in this national park. The naturalist has watched and noted the swift return of the forest, now covering 95 percent of the park. By the mid-1970s, almost 80,000 acres of the park were designated official wilderness.

"People are deceived even now by the forest," he says, adding that almost all of the park was cut over at different times. "They can't believe it was once pasture. It was logged about every 35 years. What we see isn't second growth; it could be seventh growth."

When Darwin wrote a history of Shenandoah National Park, he realized the renewal of the forest teaches an important lesson about wilderness. "Shenandoah is a recycled wilderness," he says. "In all of history, such a large area has probably never been set aside and intentionally returned to a natural state. At Shenandoah, 300 square miles were taken out of production and returned to nature. We can make a wilderness anywhere we choose. It might take 500 years in some places instead of 50, but we can do it."

"For years we've heard, 'When it's gone, it's gone forever,'" Eileen adds. "It's not necessarily true. Here we've seen its rebirth."

We part company where a stand of American chestnuts once grew. The decaying hulks of fallen trees, killed by a blight that swept through the eastern forests in the 1920s, lie among the oaks that have replaced them. The Lamberts turn down the mountain, and I head up, planning to spend the night on the other side of the range.

At the top of the Blue Ridge, I intersect the white-blazed Appalachian Trail, the same footpath I crossed in the Smokies far to the south. I follow it a short distance to Skyline Drive. The scenic highway winds the length of the park, tracing the crest of the Blue Ridge for 105 miles and joining the Blue Ridge Parkway at Rockfish Gap.

Crossing Skyline Drive, I descend into Nicholson Hollow and pass a few reminders of the people who once lived here—the rubble of stone walls, old clearing piles, and traces of roadways long abandoned. Now heavily wooded, this isolated hollow once held more than 20 homesteads. When the Park Service took over, it razed many of the existing cabins and let all but a few deteriorate. In the 1950s, the Park Service gave the Potomac Appalachian Trail Club, a volunteer organization, permission to renovate one of the original cabins to use as a shelter for hikers.

I reach the Hughes River, which is only a creek this far up in the mountains. Then I see it—the old mountain home. Corbin Cabin sits on the far bank in a grassy clearing. A stone chimney rises above cabin walls built with chestnut logs, weathered gray and snugly notched. The cabin fits, blending with the mountain setting. Quickly crossing the creek, I enter the clearing as late afternoon sun slants through a gap in the trees. Even without a fire burning, the rich aroma of wood smoke permeates the cabin. I feel as if I've returned home after a long absence.

Settling onto the porch, I sit without moving. There is nowhere else I need to go. A lassitude sets in that I'm unable to shake. At first I fight it, cutting firewood and hauling water. But soon I give in, letting time ease to a stop. I sit on the porch and stare into the woods, watching the trees slow the fall of light and listening to birdcalls and the murmur of the creek.

Next morning, in the gray light of dawn, a doe and two fawns graze their way into the clearing, ignoring my presence. One fawn, friskier than the other, gambols about with its white tail raised. Soon its mother nudges it gently back to the business of eating. The doe looks once in my direction with eyes as dark as the forest at night.

Some mountain people lived their entire lives without ever seeing a deer. In the 1930s, white-tailed deer reentered Shenandoah. They have thrived under the protection of the park, reaching a population in the thousands.

A German couple on a day hike cross the creek about noon. They look surprised to find a lone American living in a log cabin so deep in the hills. My German is no better than their English, so I'm unable to make them understand this is not my home. The woman points to her camera and asks, "Yes?" I nod, and she snaps a photo of what she must think is the hermit of Nicholson Hollow.

At night I sit by the fireplace, staring into the embers. Above the mantel hangs an old photograph of George T. Corbin, the mountaineer who built this cabin in 1909. He was married three times. His second wife died in childbirth during a winter storm. After burying her nearby, Corbin hurried down the hollow, floundering through waist-deep drifts to find milk for the newborn child.

George Corbin was the grandson of Aaron Nicholson, the ruling patriarch of this backwoods community—a place with a reputation of being too wild and rough for the sheriff to enter. The inhabitants of what some called Free State Hollow chose to keep to themselves and handle their own affairs. They also chose not to pay taxes on the corn whiskey they brewed. What they didn't drink they packed on mules across the mountain to customers in the valley. They also bootlegged a famous brandy made from Milam apples.

I pull a Milam from my pack. Small, tart, and very tasty—it was the favorite variety of the mountain people. Their orchards have now gone wild, but the apple-growing tradition continues at Mountain Green, a historic farm on the edge of the park I visited earlier.

The tangy scent of cider hung in the air as I talked with Alex Sharp, an apple grower with a pick-your-own orchard. We walked past his family's column-fronted home, its red brick the color of changing dogwood leaves. The park includes a 6,000-acre parcel once part of Mountain Green.

After talking about the apple business, the young farmer looked across his pastures rolling at the foot of the Blue Ridge. "Some people go to a place to find work," he told me. "Others say, 'This is where I live. How do I make it work?' It can be hard making a living on the land, but we have things somebody would work and save for a lifetime to have."

Leaving Mountain Green, I realized I'd been eating apples, in one form or another, all day: fried apples and dried apples, apple fritters and apple butter, fresh-pressed apple cider, and a traditional Appalachian variety called a Stayman eaten out of the hand.

At daybreak I leave Corbin Cabin, taking the trail up Nicholson Hollow. Not far from the clearing, a bear has clawed deep scratches into the trunk of a tree, scattering fresh chips on the trail. Biologists are uncertain why bears do this, perhaps only to mark their territory. Shenandoah has 300 to 600 black bears living in the park, the highest density in the country.

Red maple leaves drift from above, snagging in the dark branches of a hemlock. As the trail passes through tiers of oak trees, I listen to acorns rain down. Near Skyline Drive, I enter a clump of dogwoods where leaves as red as apple skins carpet the trail. The green of the hillside has faded like a coat of paint wearing thin, letting a bright undercoat of yellow and red show through. The Appalachian fall has arrived.

Once across the mountain crest, the footpath drops into the shadow of the main range. Pausing to inspect some bear droppings, I hear the sharp crack of a tree limb. I look downslope without seeing any movement, then search the canopy. About 75 feet up, a black bear is trying to hide its wide body behind a thin tree trunk.

"Good morning," I call up, and instantly the bear charges down the tree as fast as a fireman sliding down a pole. Down is where I am, so there's an uncertain moment when I wonder if the bear is coming toward me or trying to get away. It crashes through a limb or two on its speedy descent and reaches the bottom in seconds. Hitting the ground at a run, the bear disappears into the deeper woods.

I continue down the trail toward the clearing at the end of the road. I leave the mountains behind knowing that a place once stripped of trees, empty of wildlife, and overfarmed can be restored. The Appalachian parks have become a refuge, not only for the bear and the wolf but for the human spirit as well.

Flowing springs and abundant rainfall provide ideal conditions for moisture-loving plants. Within the park grow 47 species of mosses and ferns. Lacy streams cascade down a series of mossy drops in Whiteoak Canyon (opposite). The trail leading into the gorge passes through a grove of giant hemlocks and near six waterfalls.

FOLLOWING PAGES: A hiker leaps across boulders on the trail up Old Rag Mountain, one of Shenandoah's most popular scrambles.

On the heavily wooded slopes of Pinestand Mountain, fog drifts among the blossoming mountain laurels. The park provides habitat for more than 900 wildflower species, including the spiderwort (above).

*Friends gather around
a campfire outside
Corbin Cabin, tucked
deep in Nicholson
Hollow. George Corbin
built the dwelling in
1909 with logs cut
from once abundant
chestnut trees. The
Potomac Appalachian
Trail Club now
maintains the cabin
as a hikers' shelter.*

Split-rail fences enclose the high pasturelands bordering the Blue Ridge Parkway.

FOLLOWING PAGES: *Morning light breaks across the scenic parkway that winds 469 miles from Great Smoky Mountains to Shenandoah National Park.*

Biscayne National Park

A hint of gray on the cottony clouds promises a thunderstorm in the afternoon. For now the day is perfect, on the clear, blue-green waters of Biscayne Bay. It is the calm before the storm. Tomorrow will bring the raucous annual Columbus Day Regatta, with some 500 participating boats and another 2,000 loaded with spectators.

I have joined Christine Rogers, naturalist and park ranger, and Larry Lantz, manager of the park's concession operation, for a look around Biscayne National Park. Today there are only two or three other vessels in sight as we draw near Sands Key.

Like stepping-stones, the park's islands lure you southward from crowded Miami across the empty expanse of Biscayne Bay. These keys almost became Islandia, a resort linked by a ten-mile-long causeway to Key Biscayne. Years of struggle by those who wanted to preserve this last stretch of undeveloped South Florida coastline made possible the creation of Biscayne National Monument in 1968.

In 1980 it became a full-fledged national park that encompasses 181,500 acres, 95 percent of them underwater.

Sunrise silhouettes a lighthouse on Boca Chita Key.

by *Jennifer C. Urquhart*

MEDFORD TAYLOR

Once privately held, the island offers docking for visitors to Biscayne National Park.

From the safety of its borrowed shell a red reef hermit crab surveys the scene. As it grows, the soft-bodied crustacean seeks larger shell domiciles. Just behind it spreads a sea fan. Red mangroves (opposite) "stalk" across limestone remains of an ancient reef. Their leggy roots earn these plants the name "walking tree."

The park shelters such endangered species as the manatee, the American crocodile, and several kinds of sea turtles. It includes tropical hardwood hammocks, many miles of mangrove forest, and the farthest northern reaches of living coral reef in the mainland United States. And it offers the possibility of rare wilderness solitude on the doorstep of Miami.

"Figure to yourself a tree reversed, and standing on its summit," wrote John James Audubon, describing the red mangroves he saw in South Florida in the 1830s. Audubon well understood the importance of these peculiar, salt-tolerant trees. "Their tops afford a place of resort to various species of birds at all seasons," he wrote, "while their roots and submersed branches give shelter to...mollusca and small fishes."

The leggy, so-called "walking trees" are pioneers around here. By their way of reproducing—from seedlings dropped over the water—they build up land at the edge of the sea. The dense barrier they form absorbs the force of the fierce storms that periodically bash these coasts.

This time the mangroves seem to have come out second best. Where on my last visit I saw impenetrable mangrove forest, I now see a dismal tangle of naked brown roots and lifeless trees, slain by Hurricane Andrew in 1992.

Signs of renewal abound. At odd intervals in sheltered coves, young mangroves sprout; and the fish have not left. Donning masks and snorkels, we slip into the water and are soon peering into niches formed by the roots. Schools of juvenile yellowtail and mangrove snappers, striped sergeant majors, vivid parrotfish, and mottled scrawled cowfish move in waves, taking shelter here from predators.

"Nothing of him that doth fade," goes Shakespeare's lilting song in *The Tempest*, "But doth suffer a sea-change / Into something rich and strange." Change rules here.

A hundred thousand years ago, the sea level was much higher. These islands were themselves coral reefs. With the last ice age, the level of the sea dropped drastically, exposing the reefs to the air and killing the coral. Today's reefs lie farther offshore. Christine navigates the boat through Caesar Creek, around Adams and Elliott Keys. We head east into open water, then turn south to the mooring buoy at Elkhorn Reef.

Spanish navigators named these reefs that hug the Atlantic side of the Florida Keys the *Cabezas de los Mártires*—Heads of the Martyrs. Occasionally, navigators ventured too close and paid dearly for it. Hulks of many a ship rest on the ocean floor in the vicinity.

The Martyrs have fewer teeth than I remembered. In

Skeletal ribs of Alicia lure a scuba diver at Biscayne. The tramp steamer, which grounded on Ajax Reef in 1905 en route to Havana, offered valuable bounty for salvagers. Below, a spotted moray eel seems to stand guard. A number of such shipwrecks and intriguing sea creatures provide a rich array for today's visitors.

places, a couple of years ago, I had to suck in my stomach and swim gingerly over jagged tiers of elkhorn and staghorn corals. Now bits of coral lay strewn across a sandy ocean floor, where Hurricane Andrew had dumped them. Much of the intricate forest of elkhorn and staghorn coral, painstakingly built up over decades, had been felled in a few short hours.

Big rounded boulders of brain coral and star coral have survived, however. The sea fans, gorgonians, and sea whips wave gently in the surge; and the fish are as beautiful as ever. I float in a cloud of sapphires—blue tangs that turn gently as I pass through. A moon jellyfish, pinkish and about a foot in diameter, pulsates toward me. I swim aside to avoid its sting. Larry points at its "tummy," and it scoots away.

"Some people don't like change," Larry tells me, when we come gasping to the surface. "They like to see the same piece of coral in the same spot. The surge takes away anything that's not streamlined. That's why the elkhorn got carried

away. It's anything but stream- lined. But if something falls over, it makes a new habitat for something else."

A piece of broken coral shifts to reveal the home of a brittlestar, waving its arms at us. Nearby lies a compact, beige-colored creature, which Larry identifies as a pencil urchin. All around us we see fresh new elkhorn forming in characteristic layers atop the dead white remnants of the old.

Hurricanes are part of the natural process. Richard Curry,

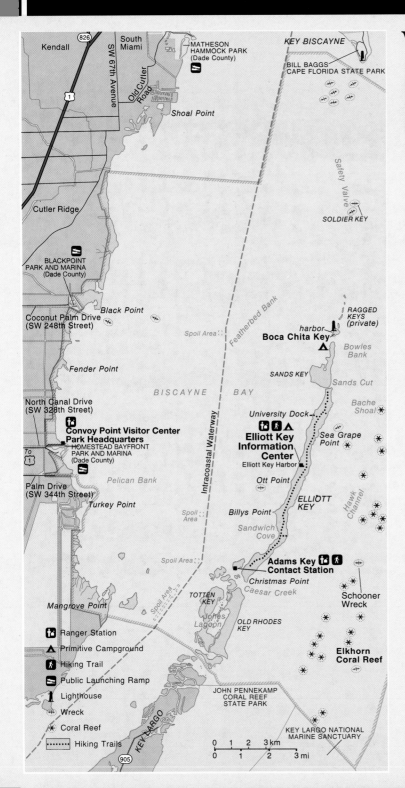

Map labels (clockwise / by region):

826
Kendall
South Miami
SW 67th Avenue
Old Cutler Road
MATHESON HAMMOCK PARK (Dade County)
KEY BISCAYNE
BILL BAGGS CAPE FLORIDA STATE PARK
Shoal Point
1
Safety Valve
SOLDIER KEY
Cutler Ridge
BLACKPOINT PARK AND MARINA (Dade County)
Black Point
Coconut Palm Drive (SW 248th Street)
RAGGED KEYS (private)
harbor
Boca Chita Key
Bowles Bank
Featherbed Bank
Spoil Area
Fender Point
SANDS KEY
Sands Cut
BISCAYNE BAY
Bache Shoal
North Canal Drive (SW 328th Street)
University Dock
Elliott Key Information Center
Elliott Key Harbor
Sea Grape Point
Convoy Point Visitor Center Park Headquarters
HOMESTEAD BAYFRONT PARK AND MARINA (Dade County)
To 1
Intracoastal Waterway
Pelican Bank
Ott Point
ELLIOTT KEY
Hawk Channel
Palm Drive (SW 344th Street)
Turkey Point
Spoil Area
Billys Point
Sandwich Cove
Spoil Area
Adams Key Contact Station
Christmas Point
Caesar Creek
Schooner Wreck
Mangrove Point
TOTTEN KEY
Jones Lagoon
OLD RHODES KEY
Spoil Area
Ranger Station
Primitive Campground
Hiking Trail
Public Launching Ramp
Lighthouse
Wreck
Coral Reef
Hiking Trails
Elkhorn Coral Reef
JOHN PENNEKAMP CORAL REEF STATE PARK
KEY LARGO
905
KEY LARGO NATIONAL MARINE SANCTUARY

0 1 2 3 km
0 1 2 3 mi

Visiting Biscayne

FLORIDA
ESTABLISHED: June 28, 1980
SIZE: 181,500 acres
HEADQUARTERS
P.O. Box 1369
Homestead, Florida 33090
Phone (305) 230-7275

HOW TO GET THERE
Take the Homestead Extension of Fla. Turnpike South to Exit 6, SW 137th Ave. (Tallahassee Road) and continue to SW 328th St. (North Canal Drive). Turn left to the park entrance at Convoy Point. From Homestead (about 9 miles) take SW 328th St. (North Canal Drive) to the park entrance. Airport: Miami.

WHEN TO GO
All-year park. The best time to visit is from mid-December to mid-April, during Florida's dry season. In summer, mosquitoes make island visits less pleasant, and fast-moving thunderstorms may occur. The Keys are accessible by boat only. A private concession operates boat trips daily, but cruises may be canceled in bad weather.

HOW TO VISIT
Private boats are allowed. Make reservations in advance for glass-bottom boat cruises and snorkeling or scuba cruises by calling Biscayne National Underwater Park, Inc., at (305) 230-1100

science coordinator for the park, explains that recovery of the red mangroves has been slow. But Andrew helped the coral reef by scouring out sediment and opening up niches. "We are seeing hard coral species that had died out long before the hurricane," he said.

Chronic problems continue for Biscayne though. They range from declining water quality, linked to Florida's ongoing water management issues, to damage to turtle grass beds and coral reefs by careless boaters.

Down the road the park faces a different kind of storm —in the form of increasing numbers of visitors. Superintendent Dick Frost told me, "We are where we are, which is just outside Miami. Eventually we are going to have thousands and thousands more people. I think the good news is that we are not yet overwhelmed by great numbers."

He added, "I think we have a little breathing room. For the Everglades it is a matter of trying to undo damage. For us it is trying to forestall and prevent damage, as we move from primarily the backyard of Miami to truly a national park that exhibits a fascinating ecosystem."

Edged by the waters of Biscayne Bay, picturesque keys (photographed before Hurricane Andrew hit) meander toward the skyline of Miami. The main threat to the park, say park officials, lies in increasing visitation.

MEDFORD TAYLOR

Everglades National Park

by Jennifer C. Urquhart • Photographed by Chris Johns

Crocodile's toothy grin emerges from shadowy red mangrove roots. Perhaps 350 of the endangered reptiles live in and near the Everglades, the nation's third largest national park.

"Holy cow, it's like snow down there," says wildlife biologist Phil Hughes. "More great egrets in the group than ibis. There's a spoonbill." The plane turns back to the east, skimming a maze of mangrove. Now there are scores of ibis below us. A manatee plows slowly through the water. Lori Oberhofer makes notations about the birds.

Farther inland we traverse the grassy sweep of Shark River Slough. An armada of tree islands, round or teardrop-shaped, sails southwestward across this mottled green-and-tan sea. As the plane dips, sunlight silvers the watery expanse, mirroring the thunderheads of a changeable autumn sky.

Motionless as statues, herons stalk prey. I spot a pair of sandhill cranes. A deer rests near a grove of trees.

We turn again toward the coast. This time we see 15 roseate spoonbills, elegant in their pink plumage.

Wildlife biologists Lori and Phil were surveying wading birds in Everglades National Park. For several days each month they flew parallel east-west transects, two kilometers apart, gathering information with which to assess conditions and trends. "This huge expanse of wilderness so near a city makes it unique," says Lori of the 1,506,539-acre national park—third largest in the nation—that sprawls at Miami's back door.

Since it was established in 1947 the Everglades has had an unusual mandate. Unlike Yellowstone, it was not intended to be a "pleasuring-ground" for the masses or to protect a stunning landscape. Its purpose is to preserve a unique ecosystem; more and more that goal seems elusive. During my sojourn in the Everglades and the adjoining Big Cypress National Preserve to the north, I would learn much about problems that confront that ecosystem and what is being done to alleviate them: from painstaking surveys such as the one we were making on this flight to high-tech computer models.

Often people define the Everglades by what's *not* here. This is not the Grand Tetons, they explain apologetically, or Yosemite—as if you somehow hadn't noticed the steamy climate, or that the saw grass prairie stretching as far as you can see could vie for flatness with the wheat fields of Kansas, and win.

"Visitors just don't understand this kind of environment," a park biologist told me. "To them, a swamp is just slog." "Besides," adds a longtime park staff member, "It's muggy, buggy, and everything here stings or bites."

Yes, there are mosquitoes, alligators, crocodiles, and snakes, too. But there are also the herons, egrets, and ibis, as well as bald eagles, palm trees and rare orchids, panthers and deer, jewel-bright tree snails, and expanses of some of the clearest water you'll ever see. Here plants and animals of the temperate and tropical zones meet at the boundaries of their ranges. Strictly speaking, only a small part of the Everglades qualifies for the designation of swamp: "a wet place, dominated by shrubs and trees." But it is *flat*. A sign along the main park road—"Rock Reef Pass, Elevation 3 Feet," it says—may make you smile, especially if you're from Colorado.

But what a difference a few inches makes. In slough-fed marshes the saw grass ripples to the horizon. Dwarf cypresses dot the expanse, like bonsai forever diminutive, stunted by nutrient-poor soils. With a little elevation, clumps of trees called bayheads take hold. On slightly higher ground, dense stands of hardwoods with melodious tropical names—gumbo-limbo, mahogany, and coco plum—form tree islands known as hammocks. Even higher, drier upland ridges—three feet high, perhaps—support pungent slash pines. At sea level on the coast grow tangles of mangrove along verdant, labyrinthine channels, where manatees browse and bottlenose dolphins cavort. South across Florida Bay's green waters, encompassing fully a third of the park, you find idyllic isles called keys.

As if to add drama, the lustrous golds, pinks, lavenders, and reds of subtropical sunrises and sunsets paint the silently moving, glassy waters of this River of Grass.

I first came to Everglades National Park many years ago, on a bright January day. Like many first-time visitors I started out on the Anhinga Trail. The park comes most into focus in winter, the dry season. Water recedes in the glades, driving animals into pools. Beside a wooden boardwalk, a couple of dozen alligators were poised motionless as logs, waiting. Turtles basked. Anhingas—called snake-birds for their serpentine necks—preened wings hung out in the afternoon sunlight. Egrets and herons stalked swarms of fish flitting through the water. Kingfishers swooped. Dragonflies darted and butterflies wafted. With a splash an otter slipped into the water.

Everywhere there was life, and a tension almost primeval. If the Grand Canyon telescopes two billion years of earth's geological story, the Everglades offers a front-row seat on the web of life. It was a visit I will never forget.

This time it was early autumn as I walked along the Anhinga Trail. The animals were less evident, dispersed throughout the park as the rainy season closed. A cricket frog called, sounding for all the world like its namesake. I strolled with John Ogden, a slender, bearded biologist then at the park's Natural Resources Center, who during nearly 25 years here studied many of the animals, observed many changes, and developed deep affection for this watery environment. "This is my favorite time of year," he said. "It's the end of the rainy season, and the marshes are full of new life. There's a peaceful look to the place."

From a distance a park airboat roared. Suddenly from nearby came a deep-throated bellow. "That's a gator answering the airboat," said John. "He's ticked off. Thinks it's a male calling—a big new alligator on the block."

Observers once marveled at the multitudes of birds here. Around the turn of the century, plume hunters nearly wiped out

Everglades National Park

To Naples
Ochopee
Tamiami Trail
Monument Lake
Big Cypress National Pres Visitor Center (Oasis)
Everglades City
Gulf Coast Visitor Center
Monroe Station
Midway
TEN THOUSAND ISLANDS
Chokoloskee Pass
Lopez
Loop Road
Loop Road Environmental Education Center
94
Huston
Chatham
Wilderness
Deer Island
BIG CYPRESS NATIONAL PRESER
New Turkey Key
Alligator Bay
Waterway
Plate Creek Bay Chickee
Toms Bight
Willy Willy
Big Lostmans Bay
South Lostmans
Lostmans
KEY McLAUGHLIN
Camp Lonesome
Highland Beach
Broad
Broad River
Harney
Tarpon Ba
Graveyard Creek
Ponce de Leon Bay
Shark
Shark River Chick
GULF OF MEXICO
Oyster Bay
Wilderness Waterway
Whitewater Bay
Northwest Cape
Joe
CAPE SABLE
Bear Lake Canoe Trail
Middle Cape
Buttonwood Canal
East Cape
Clubhouse Beach
Flamin Visitor Cen
Carl Ross Key
Sandy Key

Lake Okeechobee
FLORIDA
Atlantic Ocean
Naples
Big Cypress National Preserve
Miami
Gulf of Mexico
Biscayne National Park
Everglades National Park
Dry Tortugas National Park
Key West
0   50 km
0   50 mi

Ranger Station
Campground
Primitive Campsite
Hiking Trail
Public Launching Ramp
Wilderness Waterway and Canoe Trails
Crocodile Sanctuary (restrictions apply)

0   5   10 km
0   5   10 mi

several species, including snowy egrets and roseate spoonbills, to decorate fashionable ladies' hats. Guy Bradley, a game warden hired by the National Association of Audubon Societies, was shot by a poacher in 1905. The writer A. W. Dimock reflected in 1926 on the

From saw grass glades, cypress strands, and pine-capped ridges to estuarial mangrove forests and expanses of island-dotted Florida Bay, Everglades National Park and adjacent Big Cypress National Preserve boast a great range of environments. Though vast—encompassing more than 1,500,000 acres in the park and another 700,000 in Big Cypress—the two areas protect only about 20 percent of the original River of Grass. Once 50 miles wide and half a foot deep, it flowed more than 100 miles across South Florida.

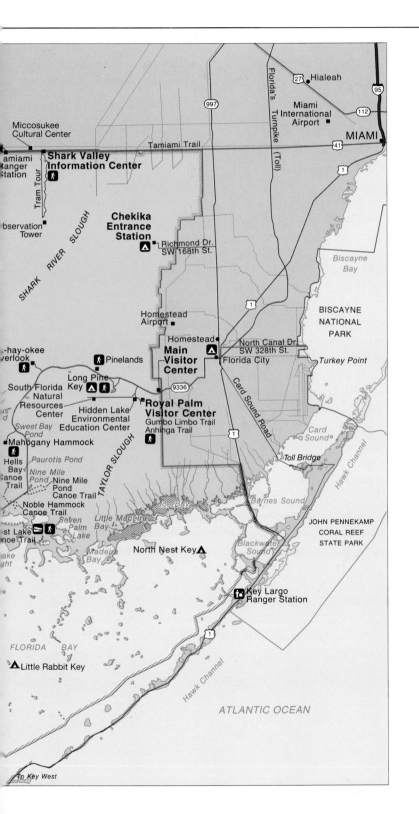

passing of the era when endless flocks of wading birds "stalked across every flat...the trees were burdened and the skies darkened by great flocks of birds of gorgeous plumage and by others of purest white, the most beautiful of created creatures."

Fashions changed. The plume trade died. Bird populations bounced back, but in recent decades numbers have again plummeted. John Ogden estimates that the number of nesting wading birds, for example, has declined 90 percent since the 1930s and 1940s. Once numerous species, such as wood storks and white ibis, no longer nest here with much success. The reasons for the decline are not entirely clear, but changing water patterns must be a large part of the cure.

Enduring swarms of mosquitoes near Flamingo Visitor Center, botanist Roger Hammer gets his reward: a delicate butterfly orchid. "I still feel," he says of the park, "that every time I go there, I can discover something." Wildlife biologist Joe Wasilewski (opposite) examines a five-year-old crocodile near the nuclear power plant at Turkey Point. Cooling canals for the facility on Biscayne Bay prove ideal breeding habitat for the rare reptiles—and help, Wasilewski thinks, to stabilize populations in the nearby Everglades.

What is clear is that the Everglades has the unenviable honor of being considered the most endangered national park. Threats come in many forms, from invasive exotic plants to mercury contamination in fish and other wildlife to diminishing water levels and the death of sea grass beds on the shallow banks of Florida Bay. "It's hard to convince people that there is a problem," said John. "It looks so peaceful. This is one of the reasons I love the Everglades, because it's a totally, totally relaxing place."

If you gaze to the horizon in the Everglades, across the rippling saw grass—called *Pa-hay-okee*, Grassy Water, by the Indians—you might imagine the tallgrass prairie of the Old West. And as surely as that once seemingly limitless expanse was tamed by barbed wire and plow, the Everglades of South Florida has been corralled by plumbing: more than 1,400 miles of it.

Once the Everglades flowed slowly south from Lake Okeechobee, some 100 miles to the north, in a shallow sheet of water 50 miles wide, to spill finally into Biscayne Bay, Florida Bay, and the Gulf of Mexico. Marjory Stoneman Douglas—long known for coining a name for that flowing water in her book *The Everglades: River of Grass*, and for her eloquence in publicizing threats to this unique ecosystem—understood its delicate balance. She likened it to "a set of scales on which the forces of the seasons, of the sun and the rains, the winds, the hurricanes, and the dewfalls, were balanced so that the life of the vast grass and all its encompassed and neighbor forms were kept secure."

For a century, Floridians have tinkered with that balance,

installing a Rube Goldberg-like array of levees, canals, and spillways, to block water here, move it there, and often simply to pour it into the sea to drain areas for people to live and for farmland, such as the huge Everglades Agricultural Area near Lake Okeechobee.

Despite appearances, South Florida is not absolutely flat. If it were, the water that makes the Everglades work in the first place would run immediately into the sea. There is an almost imperceptible downward slope from north to south, and the coastal edges of South Florida rise a little higher than the middle, like a saucer. "Water will run downhill," a colorful politician named Napoleon Bonaparte Broward was fond of saying; he ran for governor and won in 1905 on the promise of draining the Everglades, and later he breached that saucer's rim. This coastal ridge, underlaid by highly permeable limestone called Miami oolite, allows South Florida to retain rainwater and groundwater essential both for people and for the Everglades.

Mrs. Douglas understood that, claiming that 80 percent of South Florida's freshwater comes from the wet Everglades. "If you don't maintain that," she said, "it would be a desert, and we wouldn't be able to live here."

The demands of humans often appear diametrically opposed to those of the Everglades. Winter, the driest period, coincides with the tourist season and peak water usage. *(Continued on page 133)*

FOLLOWING PAGES: Don Edwards and Glen Simmons pole sleek glade skiffs modeled after traditional Seminole craft. Saddened by the decline of wildlife in the region, longtime glades resident Simmons faults "Uncle Sam and his ditch diggers" for creating South Florida's canal system.

Wielding saw grass like a wand, Marjory Stoneman Douglas can contemplate many long decades during which she presided over the defense of Florida's Everglades. "The truth of the river is the grass," she wrote in her pivotal 1947 volume The Everglades: River of Grass. *A green tree frog finds a secure niche, protected by jagged teeth that earn the grass—actually a sharp-edged sedge—its name. Security arrives less easily for the fragile Everglades, where problems find no easy solutions.*

LARRY ULRICH

Alligator peers out of lush greenery, in wait perhaps for prey. A newly hatched gator (opposite, top) hitches a ride across a duckweed-choked pond atop its mother's head. Female alligators nurture their young in a manner rare among reptiles. Largely freshwater inhabitants, alligators venture into brackish areas, such as that shown at lower left. Paurotis palms signal the transition zone where freshwater glades meet estuarial mangroves. Alligators play a key role in opening trails and clearing vegetation from ponds and water-filled depressions, important to the survival of many species during the dry season.

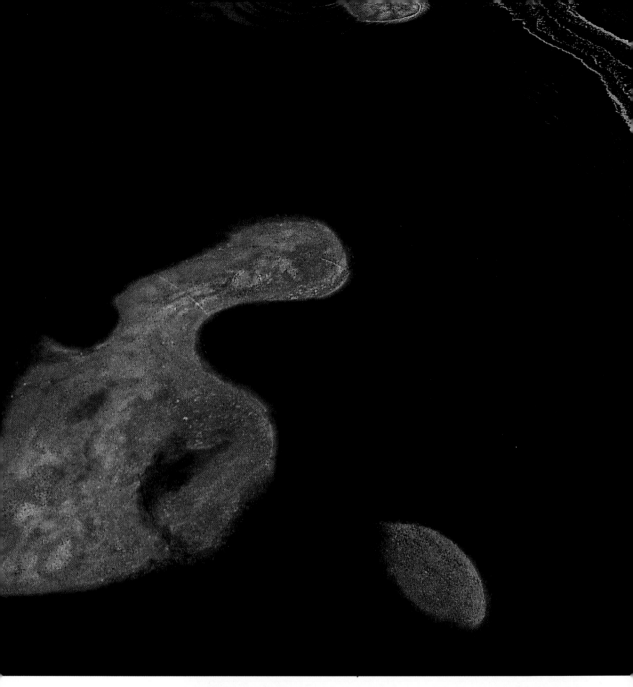

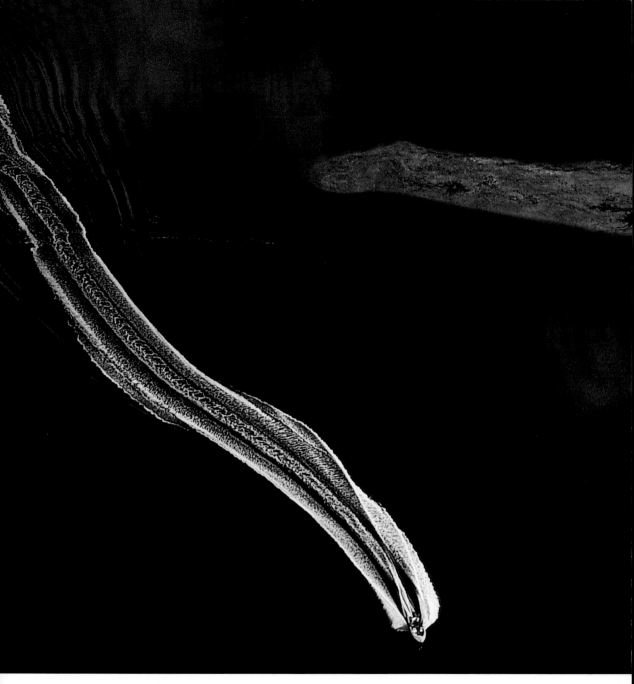

Powerboat threads sandbars in the shallow waters of Florida Bay, a favored fishing area. On Carl Ross Key, at the edge of the park, campers enjoy fishing and reading in evening's last glow. The once productive fishery of Florida Bay greatly declined in recent years, as sea grass die-offs and algal blooms clouded the crystal-clear waters.

Tricolored herons
hover over their young.
A great egret feeds
one chick (opposite,
bottom), as another
waits. While nesting
success for some birds
has plummeted in the
park, some pairs still
produce young.
Native slash pines, saw
palmettos, and cabbage
palms (opposite, top)
cap higher ridges.

FOLLOWING PAGES:
Veiled against
mosquitoes, paddlers
explore mangrove
tunnels, part of the
park's more than 100
miles of waterway.

During the wet season the problem is often how to get rid of excess water. Jim Webb of The Wilderness Society, however, doesn't see a split between human and wildlife needs.

"What's good for wood storks is good for urban rate payers," he said. "They both need clean water and plenty of it." The problem, he contends, is a water management system that functions so badly that nature suffers, and some towns on the coast are considering building desalination plants for urban water supply. "That's pretty anomalous in a place where it rains 60 inches a year," he said. "We're doing something very wrong."

If there was one constant in the Everglades in its natural state, it was change: by storm, by fire, by the unpredictability of the annual hydrological cycle. "The taming of the system, the loss of surprise and extremes," John Ogden told me, "has either driven the animals out of the system or they don't reproduce properly." Though there is long-term documentation only for the wading bird populations, John thinks that other animals have declined at about the same frightening rate. In the 1970s the Park Service established what is now the South Florida Natural Resources Center to bring scientists together to focus on the declining resources of the park and to figure out why it was happening.

Some clues are emerging, John explained. "There is a lot more information now about the dynamics of the natural system. I don't think we've fully realized, for instance, how much the food chains have changed in the last few decades." John pointed out spongy, tan stuff, algal mats floating in the water and encasing plant stems—the periphyton. Everyone knew that these micro-algae were the base of the food chain. "But it's much more complex than we thought."

Studies have revealed two major different periphyton communities. In marshes that remain dry for a long time—flooded on average only four to nine months a year—most of the periphyton consists of blue-green algae. Periphyton in wetter marshes—flooded ten to twelve months a year—has more green algae. With changes in water flow in the marshes, some areas that used to have long wet periods are drier and have blue-green instead of green algal communities.

All this might seem unimportant—until you see that in lab tests tadpoles grow slowly or survive poorly when living off the blue-green algae and on the green they flourish. "It is possible to conclude that there is less food value in the blue-green algae than the green," John said. "It may be that the total ecosystem food production has been sharply reduced because of these changes in the periphyton communities caused by reduced water flows. Yet the Everglades looks the same. The animal populations may have crashed because of something as basic as changes in algae."

With wings held aloft, a roseate spoonbill filters invertebrates and small fish out of the water and mud. Upon contact with prey, nerve endings inside its spatulate bill signal it to clamp shut. Plume hunters once targeted spoonbills for their gorgeous, rose-red breeding plumage. By the 1930s spoonbills numbered only 15 breeding pairs here. Unlike some of the park's large freshwater wading birds—the wood stork and white ibis—this mainly estuarial feeder has bounced back. Nearly 1,000 pairs now nest here.

MEDFORD TAYLOR

*Light filters through
a stand of native slash
pine, which favors
higher, drier ground.
The highest point in
the park is eight feet
above sea level.
The rocky ridges are
more vulnerable to fire
than the more moist
hardwood hammocks.
In 1992 Hurricane
Andrew snapped
off 30 percent of the
park's pines.*

A soft *kek-kek-kek* came across the water. "There's a king rail calling. Hear it?" asked John. An alligator glided by in the dark water. "A good-size one, probably a female. The old-timers say, 'Look, she's so pretty, isn't she sweet.' They mean that the female is delicate looking in a subtle sort of way, compared to a big male. She's totally at home. Moving about because it's overcast. She's happy!"

Most park visitors don't give a thought to the emotional state of a gator. Will it attack, they wonder. The gators don't bother people, John reassured a woman who hesitated, frightened to follow her husband down the Anhinga boardwalk. "But they just *love* dogs!" he added after she had left. (That's one reason no pets are permitted in the park.) Even alligators play a constructive role, though. They keep water holes open and clear of debris and vegetation around willow heads and cypress domes, providing refuges for themselves and other animals in which to survive the dry season.

They can show a surprisingly tender side, too. During courtship the male alligator may actually stroke the female's back. Females exhibit elaborate parental care, more birdlike than reptilian. They

GLENN VAN NIMWEGEN

monitor nests and listen for soft whimpers as the 30 or so eggs are about to hatch, then assist offspring in shedding egg cases. For as long as two years mothers will protect their young.

Once John and some other researchers were out in the glades on an airboat making a count of nests. Females can be aggressive if you approach their young or their nests. The crew had finished and were trying to start the boat when a female attacked. Round and round the boat she chased them, in a scene worthy of the Keystone Kops. "She was just doing her job!" chuckled John. "And finally just to make sure we understood our problem, she climbed up *over* the front of the airboat into the front seat. No, this is true," he replied to my raised eyebrow. "We actually had to climb on top of the cage over the prop to keep her from nipping us." In the end they had to poke her in the nose with a pole to move her off.

In 1897 a man named Hugh L. Willoughby journeyed across the Everglades in a canoe. In writing later of the adventure, Willoughby noted that "the skilful use of the pole is an absolute necessity in work in the Everglades." Glen Simmons wields a mean pole, and has for nearly 70 years. With bare feet planted firmly in the stern, Glen deftly nosed the narrow skiff through the mangrove. Spike rushes swished as we glided past.

I had joined him for a ride in one of his boats around Nine Mile Pond, off the park's main road. Long before there was a national park here, during the Depression, Glen took off into the Everglades. "You could make a good living here. I don't mean money. You could eat." He spent weeks at a time on these waters, hunting alligators and otters to sell, living off fish, frogs, and birds. People in this part of Florida were survivors. Life was rough. In the old days many, including Glen's mother, lived in palmetto houses with no windows. Smudge pots kept down the mosquitoes. Moonshiners, drunks, scoundrels, and just plain antisocial types: You could find them all back in the glades. "Used to be so many whiskey stills," Glen said, "they used barrel staves to mark the trail and keep from going to the wrong still.

"No fish here, I don't understand it. No gator trails or nothing," he muttered as we glided along. "Before, you couldn't hardly catch a fish for the gators."

To really see the Everglades you have to get close, and I was doing just that. In fact, I was about to land in the water. The tippy craft wobbled. I scarcely dared breathe—much less laugh at Glen's stories. His boats are really made for one person, he admitted as he warned me not to grab the saw grass to steady us. "The teeth are pointed up," he said. "If you're not careful you'll cut yourself."

At least the water's warm and not very deep, I thought. Then I saw the alligator—a nice seven- or eight-footer. Glen crooned a thin, high-pitched call. "Baby gator sound," he said. "That's the way gator hunters called them in." The gator turned and headed directly toward us.

"I don't know what he's eating, poor thing," said Glen, again noticing the scarcity of fish. I had an idea, but I kept it to myself. To my relief it turned away at the last moment.

A great blue heron lumbered into the air. The call of a limpkin came across the water, plaintive as a baby's cry. As we pulled in, still dry, to shore, several fish jumped, reassuring to Glen. One reason we had not seen many fish was that in the high-water season they disperse into the glades. There have always been natural fluctuations in the numbers of fish, biologist Bill Loftus told me at the resources center, where he studied the park's freshwater fish and invertebrates.

With his son and a teddy bear for passengers, Miccosukee Indian Kenny Cypress roars across the glades in his airboat. Miccosukees earn cash taking tourists for rides outside the park—where airboats are banned. Tribesmen also harvest palm fronds and cypress poles in Big Cypress to make traditional chickee shelters.

For decades there has been a tug-of-war between the park, the U. S. Army Corps of Engineers, the South Florida Water Management District, and others—all involved in various aspects of South Florida's water supply—over who was to have what water when. The park generally came out on the short end, ultimately becoming much drier. "As a result the animal communities out here changed quite a bit," Bill said.

Times have changed. After lawsuits and protests and more, the various groups involved in the issues hope to cooperate in a different way. "If I have to name a restoration goal," Bill stated, "it is to try to get the hydrology of the southern Everglades back to as close an approximation as possible of what it was."

Bill described a computer model that researchers have come up with of the "natural system," as it may have been at the turn of the century, before humans began meddling with it. "We have actual data on the rainfall—including extreme years, wet years, dry years, and average years. We put all those into the model and produce a series of pictures showing how, under different rainfall conditions, the system might have responded historically."

I spoke with Bob Johnson, then chief of the hydrology department at the resources center. "There once was progressive drying that is very different from what it is today," he said. The aim is to "get back to that natural timing and flow distribution and to put water back where it used to be." To Bob and his staff falls the task of designing structural changes to make that happen.

One thought gnaws at Bob: "The real question is whether or not, once you've built all these structures to move water back to where you need to in the park, there is going to be water to move." You could spend hundreds of millions of dollars to restore flow and not have enough water to do the job, because it is promised elsewhere for sugarcane fields or cities.

Early one morning I headed out from the marina at the park's Flamingo Visitor Center with wildlife specialist David Hitzig to explore some of the park's coastal areas in his outboard cruiser. We skirted Whitewater Bay, then turned up the Joe River, passing one of the park's camping platforms—called "chickees," after the thatch-roofed huts used by local Seminole-Miccosukee Indians.

At the upper end of Whitewater Bay, David took a shortcut through a bewildering maze of mangroves. The depth finder said zero. "Oh, yes, I know it's shallow," David said sympathetically to his squawking motor, which at this point was plowing mud.

After several false starts and running aground a couple of times we came out into Shark River. Ospreys, white ibis, and bald eagles all occupy the mangroves. "You'll see one eagle's nest and six ospreys' nests in close proximity," David explained. "The eagles love the ospreys because they are such good fishermen. They steal fish from the ospreys. There's another dolphin."

David told me how he likes to get people slogging in the Everglades, so they will really see its treasures—"to go into a cypress dome and find a barred owl's nest; to look for a crayfish in a pool and an orchid in a tree. They go away and say, 'My goodness, 25 feet from the road, and it's a whole different world!'"

Another afternoon I wandered along the interpretive boardwalk named Mahogany Hammock for a particular giant that is the largest mahogany in the United States. Smaller mahoganies flourished in openings yielded by downed fellows. A few birds twittered. Water dripped off glossy, tapered leaves seemingly designed to shed like a raincoat. Orchids and bromeliads, festooned on trees, took an opposite approach, capturing water in gutter-shaped leaves. Clutching host trees in a death grip, strangler figs reached for the sky. Pink-red bark peeled off the gumbo-limbos, also known as "tourist trees," after Florida's hapless sunburned visitors. Fish idled in dark solution holes, pools eaten into limestone bedrock by acidic waters.

The shade of a hardwood hammock offers some relief from the sunbaked glades, but that's where comfort ends. Mosquitoes love these hammocks. In a perverse way the mosquitoes foster a kind of camaraderie in the park as tormented sightseers are driven to a slapping tap dance.

"Mosquitoes and alligators have something in common," begins a breezy interpretive sign. "They both belong to the food web. Mosquito larvae are eaten by mosquito fish" in a "...chain that eventually ends with the alligator." Then, in a bit of salesmanship worthy of the best Florida land speculator flogging submerged acres to naive investors, the sign offers visitors a chance for free—as if they had a choice—to participate in that process: "A drop of your blood allows you to become part of this cycle of life."

Mother osprey brings home dinner for her month-old chick. Unlike bald eagles, ospreys in the Everglades have declined. From about 200 nests in 1970, the count in Florida Bay has dropped to 70 in the 1990s.

To some people the mosquito is a friend. "Thank the Lord for the mosquitoes, the world owes them a lot," wrote one naturalist-author, crediting the rapacious insect with stalling development in this part of the world. Though anthropologists have documented human activity in the region for 10,000 years, until the end of the last century people lived lightly on this watery land.

Modern development has transformed wild South Florida, and with it the Everglades. The region's ecology is deeply threatened. It seems impossible that a park as vast as the Everglades could die, but that's exactly the view I heard expressed over and over. It is a chorus that has been sung for many decades by Marjory Stoneman Douglas and others. Now a new generation of conservationists is struggling to ensure that it does not happen. Joe Podgor, then executive director of Friends of the Everglades, which Mrs. Douglas founded in 1969, is more vehement than many people I spoke with. Joe looks at the historical Everglades as a whole, arguing that the whole system, of which the park is only a small part, must be repaired.

Most people realize that the River of Grass cannot be restored to its original state. Fifty percent of it is gone. The huge Everglades Agricultural Area blocks the natural sheet flow. "To restore the original Everglades," Joe told me, "you'd have to throw out almost everyone who lives in South Florida."

Environmentalist Nathaniel Reed, then a member of the South Florida Water Management Board, has no illusions about this being a natural system. "All you need to do is fly over South Florida and you can see that," he said. "For 100 years we've been digging, dredging, and diking out there." He adds, "Man has got to be much smarter than he has been in the past. We have to temper our water use and try to re-create, in a totally managed system, some semblance of traditional flows." Accusations, counterclaims, and lawsuits continued until a tentative agreement on water quality was reached in 1993. While it pleased neither side completely, it set up goals and steps to be taken along the lines of the natural model that Bill Loftus and Bob Johnson had described to me.

Replenished largely by rainfall, the Big Cypress Swamp does not depend as much as the Everglades does upon surface flows. Even so, the two ecosystems are inextricably linked. In a way a handmaiden to the larger park, Big Cypress National Preserve was set aside in 1974 as a buffer for the wildlife and to protect the fragile ecosystem of the Everglades.

Big Cypress is beautiful on its own. Here you actually find that dark, brooding swamp that lurks in the imagination. I drove slowly, concentrating on deep ledges and potholes in the Loop Road, south of the Tamiami Trail. Spanish moss wafted from bald cypresses up to their knobby knees in dark, tannin-stained water. Bromeliads and orchids clung at odd intervals to the ghostly mahogany trees. Clear water gushed into narrow culverts on its southward journey. Suddenly I had to brake. Something dark and as long as the road was wide came out of the shadowy forest. With its powerful tail exposed and up on all fours, the alligator harked to its primitive reptilian ancestors as it strode across the road and vanished.

I would not as easily see another of the shadowy denizens of Big Cypress. The sign beside the Tamiami Trail warns "Panther Crossing Next 5 Miles." It is almost wishful thinking, the cats are so rare; but wildlife biologist Deborah Jansen sees them regularly. For the last 18 years, in both Big Cypress and in the Everglades, Deb has observed wildlife ranging from the colorful little tree snails called *Liguus fasciatus* to the endangered red-cockaded woodpeckers to her favorite, the elusive Florida panther.

I had joined Deb to track by air four radio-collared cats she has been following since 1989. Three times a week she flies over the

Sandy stretch of East Cape Sable on Florida Bay invites campers and daytime picnickers —particularly in winter when the mosquitoes and sand flies, called no-see-ums, die down. Loggerhead sea turtles nest successfully here, despite predation by raccoons.

preserve to see if they are still alive and to monitor their movements, especially during the hunting season. "After four years of monitoring," she explains, "there are indications that one panther, male number 16, has a tendency to leave the most heavily hunted portion of his home range. In this area, it may be the speed and noise of the main mode of travel—the airboat—that encourages the panther's avoidance." Hunting for deer and hogs with dogs has already been banned in the preserve. "If a cat is on a kill and is spooked by dogs, it may have to go off and hunt again. And if it's a female with kittens, that makes it all the harder for her to raise her young successfully."

From the air it's easy to distinguish the glades and marshes of Big Cypress from those of the Everglades, as if someone had drawn a line along the boundary. The preserve is crisscrossed with deep tracks gouged by swamp buggies and swaths of saw grass flattened by airboats, while the glades in the park, which allows no motorized vehicles, stretch pristine and untouched, with only narrow deer and alligator trails visible.

We headed north over cypress and pine forest. Except for a few

JOHN SHAW

strands—long, narrow stretches of trees growing along a slough—outside the preserve, the huge, old-growth bald cypresses were felled long ago. From the plane, I felt that I could almost touch the tree-tops. Deb's receiver beeped like a Geiger counter. "That's number 23—Annie," she said. Deb had actually seen her the week before, but today the cat was resting in a stand of pines.

We passed over the drilling rigs at Raccoon Point Oil Field, one of two areas in the preserve with active wells. Again the receiver beeped wildly. "That's number 42—Junior. He was born in the Everglades and came up here to find the girls."

Now we were flying over an inholder's camp, one of a few left in the preserve. Once there were nearly 300 hunting camps. Only those with actual title to the land remain now. "He's a nice guy," Deb said of the owner of this one. "The cats ate a wild hog he had been feeding. Deer are probably preferred, but hogs are easier to catch by the young, inexperienced panthers," Deb told me. "They see a sow with a bunch of piglets: tiny morsels running behind her."

No matter how you look at it, the cats are controversial. Only 30 or so remain in the wild. Their problems go beyond vanishing

Tannin-darkened water reflects ghostly gray bald cypresses in Big Cypress National Preserve. Young sabal palms sprout low in the forest, while bromeliads, or air plants, occupy various levels. The interior of such cypress strands retains moisture during the dry season that supports a rich variety of plant life.

Exotic dinner rewards an anhinga that has nabbed a walking catfish, a species not endemic to the region. Many such exotics flourish in the Everglades, providing food for many animals. Some new arrivals seem to endure environmental changes better than do native fish. Scientists do not yet fully understand the impact of the new fish on native species.

habitat and being struck by cars on the highway. Biologists aren't certain that the Florida panther is even a separate subspecies. Its characteristic cowlick and kinked tail are marks of inbreeding. Other genetic disorders such as hereditary heart disease and feline immune system deficiencies are showing up. A plan to introduce genetic material from western cougars into the Florida panther population has stirred more debate about their future.

As much as Everglades National Park focuses on its natural ecosystem, Big Cypress copes with human activities within its environment. The 728,000-acre preserve was born of compromise—with hunters, oil interests, Native Americans, and others—and it continues to juggle diverse, sometimes contradictory, demands on its resources: What do you do, for instance, about feral hogs that ravage nests of alligators and other animals and root up young plants, but are also choice prey for hunter and panther?

Fred Dayhoff has no problem with hunting or with airboats or swamp buggies in Big Cypress, if it's done right. Fred comes from a long line of hunters who moved into Florida in the 1840s, following the game. He built his first swamp buggy when he was 13 or 14 years old. What Fred does have a problem with is a handful of froggers who take as much as 600 pounds of frogs a night, then sell them piecemeal to restaurants. Frog hunting is allowed in the preserve, but not for commercial use. Those few individuals who take so many and sell them deprive birds and other wildlife that depend on the frogs.

DAVID SMART / DRK PHOTO

He also has a problem with hunters in airboats who will run down a deer, shoot an arrow into it, and call it sport. "When you get mechanized hunting, some people get crazy," he said. "There must be a magnetic field that sucks their brains out the second they hit the Loop Road."

One morning he guided his airboat south from his house on the Loop Road and into Dayhoff Slough. "I don't know if the slough was named after me, or I after the slough," he joked. "We always used to call it Limpkin Slough."

Talk ceases on an airboat. I had donned ear protectors against the roar of the airplane engine that powers the high-rigged contraption, invented for just such terrain. I could look and point, though, and sometimes we stopped to consider the scene.

We sped across the saw grass. Fred could probably go through here blindfolded. He used to have to find his way in the dark. For many years he was a park ranger, chasing down poachers or other kinds of renegades. Red-shouldered hawks and vultures dipped and glided as they scanned for likely prey. A snail kite teetered on a dwarf cypress. On willows just above the waterline hung clusters of apple snail eggs, which produce the favored food for snail kites. Star-like swamp lilies were scattered across the prairie. Some had been clipped off. Deer love them, Fred told me. A deer started ahead of us and bounded frantically away through the water. Dragonflies, other insects, and spiders kicked up as we cruised along.

A least bittern flew up out of the saw grass. "Rare to see," said Fred. There's only a shadow now, he told me, of the wildlife he remembers when he was growing up. "I've seen this prairie covered with birds. Over half a mile of birds feeding. And if the wind was right you'd hear 'em. The ibis going *um, umm, umm*, and the clacking of the wood storks' beaks. It's something you thought would never disappear."

I headed south again, to Florida Bay and the farthest limits of Everglades National Park. I wanted to spend a night on Carl Ross Key, a designated campsite seven miles offshore and breezy enough to be mosquito free. Avid fisherman Alex Carpenter had agreed to run me out to the island in his fishing boat. He pointed out, "See the nervous water," where schools of mullet stirred. While I scanned the sky and horizon for birds, Alex sought signs of snook or tarpon and grabbed his fishing pole to cast at any promising shadow.

We skirted the Oyster Keys—where the unfortunate Guy Bradley lost his life—then turned across the bay to Sandy Key rookery, where Audubon found the air "darkened by whistling wings." Alex dropped me off on the crescent beach of adjacent Carl Ross.

I was alone until morning, with a delicious sense of solitude—and total security. There weren't even raccoons on my island to raid my food. I wandered around and watched sanderlings scooting along, dipping bills into the sand and dancing with little wavelets that lapped the shore. Waves of plovers whirred nearby. Later, after dinner in my tent, I dozed off, listening to fish leaping and slapping the water. In the middle of the night a storm, with lightning and thunder and teeming rain, blew through. I enjoyed the show from my snug, dry tent. As the sun came up rosy and bright, I wished for good fortune to dawn over this special, fragile corner of the world.

Before I left Florida I visited briefly with Marjory Stoneman Douglas, frail but still forthright at age 103. Was she hopeful about saving the Everglades? Her spirit was contagious. "It's not a question of being hopeful," she replied. "I say it's got to be done!"

FOLLOWING PAGES: *To hop or not to hop: A tree frog clings to its saw grass perch, seemingly oblivious to an approaching water moccasin— and possible doom. In the ongoing struggle for survival, myriad creatures in the Everglades open wide a window on life's intricate web.*

Seeking sibling support, two young tricolored herons teeter unsteadily on a branch. Unable to fly yet, the two still depend on parents for food. A yellow rat snake slithers through palm fronds. The fierce-looking snake actually poses no threat, helping instead to keep rodent populations in check. A bromeliad blooms in Big Cypress National Preserve. Close observation in the Everglades and Big Cypress reveals many microenvironments.

Visiting Everglades

FLORIDA
ESTABLISHED: December 6, 1947
SIZE: 1,506,539 acres
HEADQUARTERS
40001 State Road 9336
Homestead, Florida 33034
Phone (305) 242-7700

HOW TO GET THERE
Take U. S. 1 south from Miami to Florida City, then go west on Fla. 9336 (formerly Fla. 27) to the Main Visitor Center, about 50 miles from Miami. If you are coming from west of Miami, take U. S. 41 (Tamiami Trail) to Fla. 29, then head south to Everglades City. Airports: Miami and Naples.

WHEN TO GO
Everglades has two seasons: dry from mid-December through mid-April and wet the other eight months of the year. The park is open daily, year-round, but most activities are scheduled during the dry season. Some facilities and activities are limited or closed in the off-season—from May 1 to mid-December. Hot, humid weather and clouds of mosquitoes can make visitors very uncomfortable during the wet season.

WHAT TO DO
Swimming is not advised at this park. Alligators and snakes live in the ponds. Insect repellent is essential year-round. During the dry season, reservations are advised for guided tours.

Whether you have time for a short visit or a longer stopover, the **Anhinga Trail** at **Royal Palm Visitor Center** is a must. The **Mahogany Hammock** trail, which takes you into the humid, subtropical forest, is also interesting, as is **Pay-Hay-Okee Overlook,** for an expansive view of the glades.

Park naturalists lead nature tours throughout the year. In the dry season "**swamp tromps**"

across marsh and hammock are favorites. In the northern part of the park the guided **Shark Valley Tram** cruises a 15-mile loop. Or you can rent a bike and pedal on your own.

Boat trips are available out of **Flamingo** and **Everglades City**. Florida Bay offers good fishing—for which a Florida license is required. Opportunities for canoeing and motorboating include short circuits around **Nine Mile Pond** and **West Lake**. Or you can spend several days camping on platforms called chickees along the **Wilderness Waterway**, which meanders 99 miles along mangrove-lined channels, from **Flamingo Visitor Center** to **Gulf Coast Visitor Center**. Camping permits are required. Houseboats are also available for rent.

Big Cypress Preserve

FLORIDA
ESTABLISHED: October 11, 1974
SIZE: 728,000 acres
HEADQUARTERS
HCR 61, SR Box 110
Ochopee, Florida 33943
Phone (941) 695-2000; 695-4111 (Visitor Center)

HOW TO GET THERE
Situated between Miami and Naples and adjacent to the Everglades, Big Cypress extends north across U. S. 41 (Tamiami Trail) and I-75 (Alligator Alley).

WHAT TO DO
There is a Visitor Center at Oasis Ranger Station on the Tamiami Trail. A slow drive along the **Loop Road**—very rough in parts—offers views from within a bald cypress swamp and excellent birding opportunities. Hunting, fishing, and off-road vehicles—with permits—are allowed within some areas of the preserve.

Topping the park's avian food chain, the bald eagle maintains a stable population of about 50 nesting pairs.

Dry Tortugas

Designed for
450 guns,
Fort Jefferson
harkens to
Civil War times
and its renown
as the "Gibraltar
of the Gulf."

MATT BRADLEY

National Park

by Tom Melham

I t was January of 1861, months before the attack on Fort Sumter. The Confederacy did not yet exist. Secession had begun, however, and throughout the South, state militias were moving to take charge of federal forts. A gunboat representing the state of Florida neared Fort Jefferson, at the extreme end of the Florida Keys, demanding its surrender. Union commander Maj. Lewis G. Arnold considered his situation: He had several dozen soldiers, in a fort begun 15 years earlier but still far from completion, and

already its walls were cracking. Only a handful of cannon had arrived, not one of them in working order. His response was swift and daring: If the intruder did not leave in ten minutes, Arnold warned that he would "blow his ship out of the water." The Southerner looked again at Fort Jefferson's imposing bulk—and sped off without firing a shot.

Like Arnold's bluff, the fort itself would prove to be both a bold stroke and something of a sham. It was the physical manifestation of a grand military design that had been rooted more in fantasy than in reality.

Once dubbed America's "Gibraltar of the Gulf," Fort Jefferson now is a national park—one of the nation's newest, and in some ways its strangest and most remote. It spans a hundred square miles,

Interior views include cloister-like archways, a barrel-roofed arsenal, and a memorial to Dr. Samuel Mudd.

almost all of them underwater. Less than one square mile juts above high tide: the combined area of seven sand-and-coral islets known as the Dry Tortugas. (The name alludes to the isles' total lack of freshwater and an abundance of sea turtles, *tortugas* in Spanish.) They are the *real* end of the Florida Keys—70 miles west of Key West, 90 miles north of Cuba, and 120 miles from the Florida mainland. You get there by

Armadas of sooty terns besiege Bush Key every April, dining on fish and nesting directly on the warm sand.

TOM MELHAM, NGS STAFF; MARTY CORDANO / DRK PHOTO (OPPOSITE)

Leaning lean-to —the remains of a research lab— and toppled trees testify to past tempests on Loggerhead Key, largest of seven islets that make up Dry Tortugas.

boat or—if you're like me—by floatplane, out of Key West.

The first 15 minutes, you see nothing but open sea. Then, briefly, the scattered mudflats and mangroves of the Marquesas. Twenty minutes more of ocean in every direction pass before you spot what could be a six-sided, red-brick prototype for the Pentagon, rising from the sea like a mirage. It is hollow, horizontal, and so massive that four of its sides actually over-

flow the key on which it stands. Tiers of brick arches, reminiscent of a Roman aqueduct, comprise its inner perimeter. The pilot circles, and again you see only ocean from horizon to horizon. And you wonder, why *here?* Why build such an enormous fort in a place so disembodied from any mainland?

For answers, you need to go back a century and a half, to the America of the 1840s. It was a time of optimism, opportunity, and rapid economic growth. Expansionism was rife; Texas had broken from Mexico, pioneers were pushing into Kansas and Nebraska Territories. Americans dreamed of a single nation spanning the continent (and even extending into Central America).

Many also feared foreign intrusion, while burgeoning commerce along the Mississippi Valley underlined the Gulf of Mexico's growing importance to the nation. Military planners devised a baseline of defense: A string of coastal forts from Maine to Texas would secure the Republic. Linchpin and largest component of this system would be Fort Jefferson, 16 million bricks arrayed in a beefy hexagon half a mile in perimeter, the walls 8 feet thick and 50 feet high. It would protect the sea traffic to the Gulf of Mexico.

Detractors called the site indefensible and inconsequential. Backers considered it strategic. First, the Dry Tortugas bordered the 90-mile-wide Straits of Florida, principal sealane linking the Atlantic with the Gulf. More important, they ringed a major deepwater harbor, one roomy enough to accommodate the nation's entire mid-19th-century navy. While no fort's guns could hope to control the Straits, they could command the Tortugas harbor. Fortify that har-

bor and fill it with warships, and the resident fleet could sally forth at will, ensuring American control of the Straits. Lose the opportunity, and some other power might occupy the Tortugas—and put the nation's Gulf traffic at risk.

The planners, however, overestimated foreign interest in the Straits and underestimated the daunting logistics involved in defending them. Cement, brick, stone, lumber, even sand and water had to be imported, as did labor and food —from as far afield as New York and Maine, all at great expense. Workers were hard to recruit and harder still to keep in the hot, isolated, and fever-ridden Tortugas.

Construction—and Congressional appropriations— dragged on nearly 30 years, turning the colossal fort into a colossal boondoggle. Founda-

Part of a 2,500-member colony, a brown noddy tern nests in shrubs and scrub. Songbirds and other migratory birds frequent the Tortugas, which lie on a major flyway to South America.

tions failed; walls cracked. The fort was too difficult and expensive to build, so remote as to be untenable, and it guarded a "prize" no one really wanted. It was never completed, and it never experienced combat.

The Civil War was its undoing, not by direct attack but because the introduction in 1861 of rifled cannon—which could breach even Jefferson's mammoth walls—rendered this and every other masonry fort obsolete. America's Gibraltar became its Devil's Island, a disease-prone prison mostly for military deserters.

Its most famous inmate, however, was civilian. Dr. Samuel Mudd, convicted as one of ten "Lincoln Conspirators," had set the broken leg of John Wilkes Booth—without knowing of Lincoln's death.

The Army abandoned Fort Jefferson in 1874, briefly returning in 1898 with the Navy during the Spanish-American War. Ten years later, the Tortugas were made a bird preserve. In 1935 they passed to the National Park Service as a national monument; upgrading to national park status came in 1992.

Today's attractions—apart from the fort—are the birds and the marine life. These sandy islets provide nesting sites for sea turtles—especially loggerheads—as well as for thousands of sooty and noddy terns. Also, they lie on major flyways.

Birders, says park supervisor Wayne Landrum, "can see as many as a hundred species in three days." For divers and snorkelers, Tortugas offers "the best living coral reef system in the continental United States, period. It's a remote area, so it's less impacted than the rest of the Florida Keys. The coral reefs are more pristine here."

Regulations also are stiffer. Just up the Keys at Biscayne National Park, spearfishing, lobstering, and commercial fishing all are legal. Not so at Fort Jefferson. "This is a reserve. Everything is allowed to develop and grow here. We have the biggest lobster, the best sportfishing."

Most visitors come through Key West, often just for the day. Overnight camping is possible but limited; campers must bring all their needs, even water, and pack everything out. There are no concessions, no stores, no supplies for 70 miles. Many find that off-putting. But to others, this gulfside reserve is a refreshing departure from easy-access, heavily visited parks. The very isolation that doomed it as a fort, some feel, makes it a great national park.

The Army's loss, you might say, is our gain.

Visiting Dry Tortugas

FLORIDA
ESTABLISHED: October 26, 1992
SIZE: 64,657 acres
HEADQUARTERS
P. O. Box 6208
Key West, Florida 33041
Phone (305) 242-7700 (Everglades NP)

HOW TO GET THERE

Access by boat or seaplane from Marathon, Key West, or Naples, Florida.

WHEN TO GO

April-May is prime time for birders. Snorkeling is best in summer. June-November is tropical storm season; December-March is unpredictable. No housing, food, or water are available, so bring everything you need, and plan to take it with you when you leave.

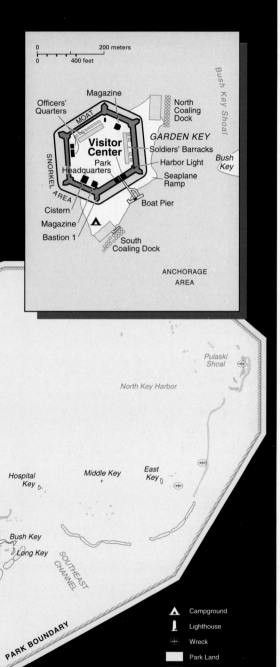

Virgin Islands National Park

by Tom Melham • Photographed by David Doubilet

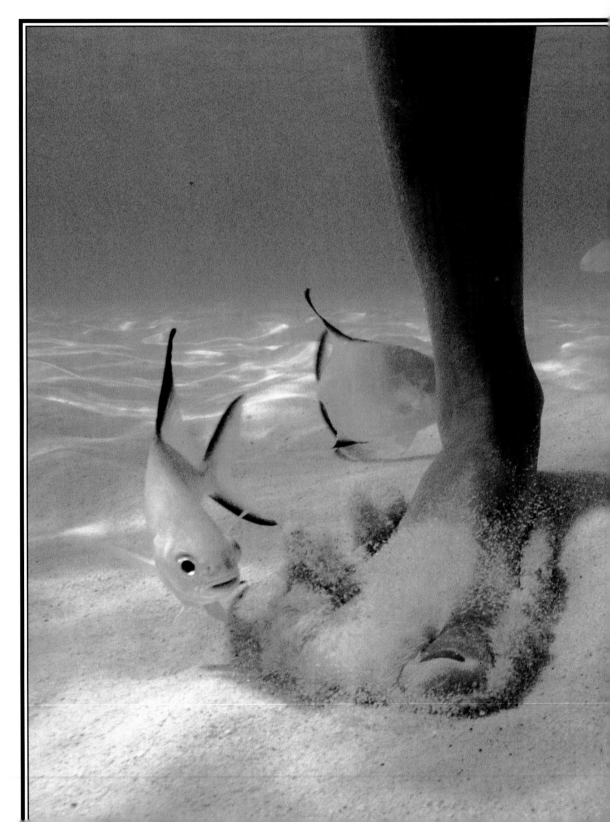

Like puppies underfoot, adult palometas dog the steps of a human visitor to St. John, U. S. Virgin Islands. They seek invertebrate snacks amid sandy debris stirred up by passing toes.

Warm, turquoise waters. Secluded sand beaches as white and powdery as moondust. Forested hillsides rising jumbled and green from the scalloped shore to the Caribbean's neon sky. In short, a tropical island paradise. Amid this shorts-and-sandals Eden, the uniform so familiar to Yosemite or Yellowstone—green dungarees, taupe shirt, flat-brimmed Stetson—seems positively alien. Park rangers *here?* You mean *this* is a national park?

Indeed it is. About half of St. John, the smallest, steepest, and least developed of the three major U. S. Virgin Islands, has been parkland since 1956, when Laurance Rockefeller gave much of his extensive holdings on the island to the federal government, and President Dwight D. Eisenhower signed Virgin Islands National Park into being. Six years later a marine addition—5,650 acres of offshore reefs and sand bottom—nearly doubled the park's original size.

Yet even today Virgin Islands National Park suffers something of an identity crisis. For although more than a million vacationers flock here yearly, says Chief of Interpretation Chuck Weikert, "many don't even know they're entering a national park."

But then VINP doesn't leap out from its surroundings the way, say, Great Smoky Mountains does from Gatlinburg's glitz. Nor does it possess Yellowstone's telltale tollbooths, nor even the solid, predictable entryways that have become a National Park Service hallmark, coast to coast. Explains VINP research biologist Caroline Rogers, "There's no entrance to this park. We're on an island, with 360-degree access by boat. People can just sail in, spend a week, and leave—and never see a Park Service sign, never see the Visitor Center, never know they're in a park."

Landlubbers also can be blissfully ignorant, thanks to this park's understated presence. For one thing, though the Visitor Center is located on St. John, the headquarters lies off-island, on citified St. Thomas. For another, the existence of numerous private holdings on St. John makes it impractical to post signs every time a road enters or leaves the park. The result: For most visitors, actual park boundaries remain out of sight and out of mind.

St. John's roads have a flavor all their own. More reminiscent of Le Mans than of Lynchburg or La Jolla, they're narrow, with steeper switchbacks and tighter hairpin turns than any highway on the U. S. mainland. Lightweight four-wheel-drives, short of wheelbase and not too wide, are the transportation of choice. Adding to this island's exotic feel, local regulations—unlike those of any other area under the American flag—dictate that you drive on the *left*.

The island is small, a bit over 19 square miles in area, with the park's landed portion about 10. "Look at a map," says Caroline Rogers, "and you can't even find it. The words 'St. John' always take up more space than the island itself."

It also is remote, lying nearer Venezuela than Miami. More than 80 percent of its surface exceeds a 30 percent grade. Much of it is densely forested. Paved roads and unpaved trails abound, yet beaten paths are few—largely because dramatic bays, ridges, and other natural features tend to subdivide and seclude, dispersing the human traffic. Many sites and even beaches remain uncrowded. No high-rises stud these shores; numerous stretches of unbroken green foster images of solitude and that rarest Caribbean entity: an unspoiled retreat. St. John may not be pristine—no Caribbean island is that—but it remains largely uncluttered and serene.

Similarly, its national park has an unstructured feel; many natural, historic, and scenic attractions are marked minimally or not at all. They're just there, waiting to be discovered and experienced, firsthand. Spot the roadside ruin of a plantation-era estate—or an alluring forest trail or especially idyllic strand—and often you need only pull off the road to enjoy it. In some places, your car will be alone or nearly so. The same for your beach towel.

Most visitors, of course, come for St. John's most obvious assets: its beaches and bays, ideal for all sorts of water sports. Such attractions, among others, led Laurance Rockefeller to build his expansive and legendary Caneel Bay resort here. Yet similar seaside pleasures may be had at many another Caribbean isle. What sets St. John apart is its surprising diversity—both above and below sea level—despite its diminutive size. Though it lacks true rain forests, rivers, or barrier reefs, the island remains a small wonder, boasting at least a taste of most everything else the Caribbean offers.

Ecologist and resident Gary Ray considers it "all-around, the most blessed of the Lesser Antilles"—that curve of West Indian landfalls that sweeps east and south from Puerto Rico to the Venezuelan coast. "Some islands are mountainous, with magnificent rain forests and beautiful topography. But they're usually so steep that there's very little shelf offshore, not much coral reef or beach. Others have lots of reefs but are extremely flat. St. John really does combine those two features better than any other island in the eastern Caribbean. It has it all."

Here, coastal waters run the gamut from colorful coral reefs to bleak but important sand flats, from rocky shallows teeming with schools of fry to submerged meadows of sea grasses. Terrestrial habitats range from subtropical moist forest—not quite as wet as tropical rain forest—through mangrove, marsh, and various dry forest habitats to cactus-studded scrub. Nearly 800 species of plants grow on this tiny island, says Gary—including more woody plants than occur throughout the continental United States and Canada combined.

Such biological diversity is especially startling given the Caribbean's history of exploitation since the arrival of Columbus. (The great navigator, incidentally, passed close by St. John on his

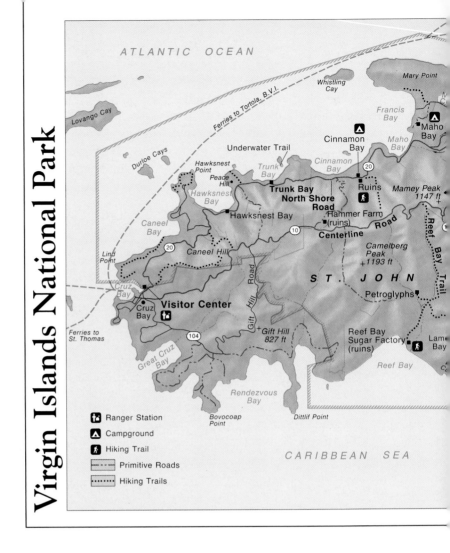

second voyage, in 1493; it was uninhabited.) Colonization brought piracy and, later, Danish planters and West African slaves, who cut the forests, terraced the hills, and raised such valued crops as sugarcane, cotton, and indigo. Subsistence agriculture and the introduction of various domestic animals also altered these islands greatly. But St. John's ruggedness and small size made it a poor candidate for prolonged commercial farming, and so despoilation here was less than it might have been. Although its virgin forests—like those of every other Caribbean isle—eventually were felled, the clearing occurred in stages, enabling nearly all native plant species to survive.

Gary, botanist Eleanor Gibney, and I are standing on a ridge of the Bordeaux Mountains, which peak out at 1,277 feet, the island's high point. It is one of St. John's wettest areas, home to some of its best examples of subtropical moist forest. Like pilings, dark, dank tree trunks hem us in, stretching from forest floor to dense canopy 60 or even 80 feet up, blotting out the sun. Even so, this is no mature climax forest. The mix of species is right, Gary explains, but the trees may have only half the girth of their forebears centuries ago.

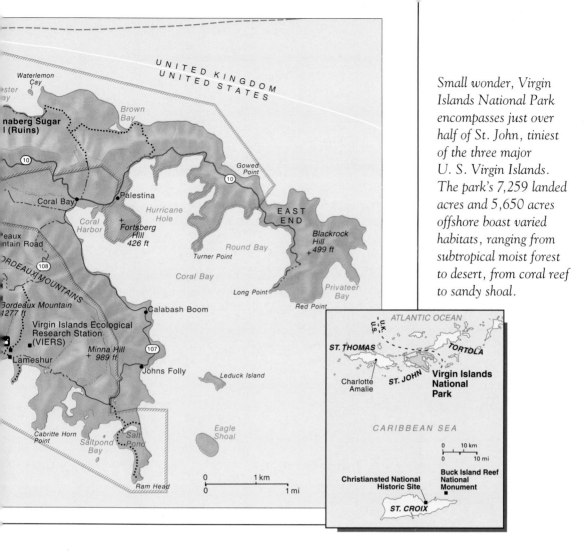

Small wonder, Virgin Islands National Park encompasses just over half of St. John, tiniest of the three major U. S. Virgin Islands. The park's 7,259 landed acres and 5,650 acres offshore boast varied habitats, ranging from subtropical moist forest to desert, from coral reef to sandy shoal.

Though much of this ridge has gone uncut for 150 years, its recovery cycle is nearly twice as long. At least another century must pass before these growths approximate the forests Columbus saw.

To my eye they're just trees, none of them remotely familiar. Some are smooth-barked, others rough; some have glistening, over-size leaves while their neighbors put forth smaller, totally different offerings. For all I can tell, each individual could be a separate species. Gary points out aerial roots of strangler figs and other vine-like growths straggling through the understory, then a West Indian locust, known for its fine hardwood—and pungently aromatic fruit that inspired the West Indian moniker, "stinkin' toe tree." Eleanor identifies other species, including one member of the holly family and one of myrtle. Both occur commonly on this ridge—but nowhere else on the island. Near this spot a few weeks earlier, she discovered an orchid that until then had been unknown to St. John.

"You find so many things up here that you just don't see any-where else," she marvels. "This mountaintop was never in agricul-ture. They took the biggest things out. But if they had cut it all at once, many of these species never would have come back." Yet she quickly adds that this stretch of moist forest is not the island's sole botanical prize, nor even its most fascinating one.

"Drier areas have the really unique vegetation. Out of the 16 plants on St. John that are considered rare and endangered, 11 are found only in the more arid parts of the island," Eleanor explains.

Such areas receive less than 40 inches of rain yearly. Depending on variations in rainfall, altitude, and exposure, the plants form anything from canopied forests to spiny thickets to sparse collections of wind-carved coastal hedge—all different formations that fall under the botanical heading of "dry tropical forest." It is Gary's specialty, and Eleanor's passion.

While it contains prized hardwoods such as ironwood and lignum vitae, says Gary, it remains "a very much unloved forest type. To most people, dry forest is just *bush*, something to hit with a machete. It's thorn, it's cactus, it's nasty. It's there to be cut down and improved upon"—especially since it occurs mainly on lower, flatter elevations that are prime areas for agricultural, residential, or commercial development.

To botanists, however, St. John's dry forest is a treasure. "You really have to see other islands to realize what we've got: continuous, well-recovered dry forest that is *protected*," explains Gary. "Everywhere else you find a good piece of it, usually it's not protected, and you know it's only a matter of time. In ten to fifteen years, most of those places will get exploited in some manner, grazed or subdivided or converted or what-have-you. Even now you go from island to island in the Lesser Antilles, and the dry forest is just gone. Totally wiped out. Or so fragmented or altered that its ecological processes and species interactions have been diminished. Except here, where some has managed to remain through historical accident."

Its rarity, he argues, makes it a far more urgent concern than, say, the more common and higher altitude moist forest. "The thing is, we know so little about it. Insects, for example—we estimate that 4,000 to 10,000 insect species may exist on this island. For all we know, hundreds may be endemic, may live nowhere else. And yet there are only a few insect collections; we know only a fraction of what's here. If the dry forest is allowed to disappear, many species could be wiped out. I think it's a crime to burn up the library before you read the books."

Among those at risk are migratory songbirds such as warblers, which shuttle between the American mainland and the Caribbean. Some of them rely at least seasonally on the tropical dry forest. About 13 different warbler species use St. John either as a stopover or endpoint, giving this island one of the highest warbler densities in the Caribbean. "This park is one of their last refuges," says Gary. "We tend to think of it as mostly a marine park. But eventually, when we understand the dry forest ecosystem, I believe we'll realize just how valuable Virgin Islands National Park is. I think its value on the terrestrial side is going to outstrip that on the marine side."

For now, though, most park visitors—human ones, anyway—focus on St. John's seaside charms. They come to sail, to windsurf, to snorkel or scuba dive, or simply to work on their suntans. Snorkelers especially favor the island's more accessible and varied North Shore, where numerous small bays offer their own particular attractions.

Trunk Bay, for example, boasts not only a stunning beach of flour-fine sand but also some coral reefs, complete with an underwater trail marked by instructive signs placed on the seafloor. Here, visitors glide among star and brain corals, past delicately branched staghorn and elkhorn corals, in search of striped sergeant majors, foureye butterflyfish, and other colorful denizens of the reef.

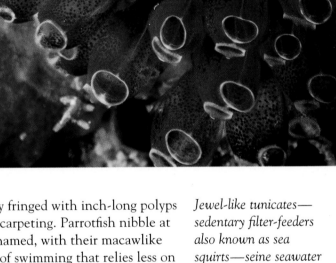

Sea whips waft back and forth in the surge, while tube sponges show their pastel reds, blues, and purples. Pillar corals put forth fingerlike columns so thickly fringed with inch-long polyps that they seem sheathed in deep-pile carpeting. Parrotfish nibble at algae-encrusted coral. They are well named, with their macawlike hues, their beaky snouts, and a mode of swimming that relies less on tail-thrusting and more on fluttering pectoral fins like tiny wings.

Absolutely teeming with life, coral reefs are considered the oceanic equivalent of tropical rain forests. They are complex and diverse ecosystems, marked by immensely varied biological niches filled with an abundance of different species. Compared to dramatic wall and barrier reefs, Trunk Bay seems scattered and patchy, more rock garden than massive forest. Even so, it offers snorkelers a solid introduction to the fascinating textures, colors, and creatures that make up coral's magical realm.

Several coves westward, in Scott Bay, the bottom seems empty by comparison. Snorkel here and you'll find no hard reef, only acres and acres of bare sand tufted with widely scattered smudges of algae.

But soon, rounded, tawny shapes materialize from the hazy edge of visibility: a trio of sea turtles! (Continued on page 180)

Jewel-like tunicates—sedentary filter-feeders also known as sea squirts—seine seawater for meals of plankton as they cling to a coral overhang.

FOLLOWING PAGES: Sprawling eastward from the principal town of Cruz Bay, VINP takes in thickly forested slopes, myriad coves, and coral-buttressed shores.

TOM BEAN

Soft Corals
Soft branching cor
shape of plu

Sugary sand and azure
water make Trunk Bay
St. John's most popular
beach. Just offshore,
markers on the seafloor
tell snorkelers about
reef life (opposite).

FOLLOWING PAGES:
Winter swells bring a
rare surf to Trunk
Bay—and delight to
visiting youngsters.

*Dry but not destitute,
the Ram Head area
(right) offers desertic
beauty and solitude.
Among its ark of
colorful species:
turk's cap cactus in
fruit (below) and a
finger-size frangipani
caterpillar (bottom).*

TOM MELHAM, NGS STAFF (ABOVE, BOTH); TOM BEAN (RIGHT)

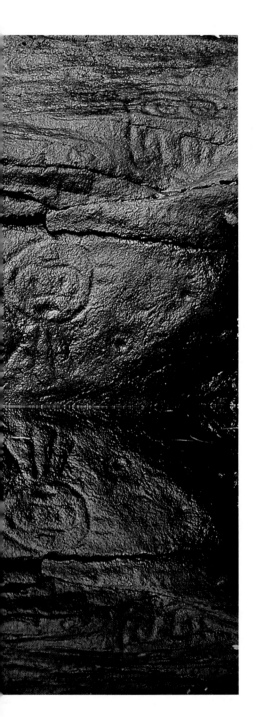

Ghostly memoranda from prehistory, petroglyphs grimace at the edge of a basalt pool just off Reef Bay Trail. A stylized cross (left) prompts speculation that Christianized slaves from West Africa etched the rock art, but experts usually credit ancestors of native Taino Indians. More recent artifacts—such as the 18th-century ruins of a Danish sugar mill on Peace Hill (above)—attest to the island's colonial past.

TOM MELHAM, NGS STAFF (ABOVE LEFT); TOM BEAN (BELOW)

Jungly second-growth forests recall St. John's original appearance, before Danish colonists and West African slaves clear-cut it into sugar plantations. But among native kapok, bay rum, and West Indian locust trees sprout exotics such as this massive genip and shrublike limeberry. Similarly, wildlife today reflects a mix of Old World and New: African millipedes commonly called gongolo "worms" and golden-orb spiders (top, opposite). Orchids include the endemic Oncidium variegatum *(below).*

Slowly digging in, a southern stingray's rippling mantle scoots aside underlying sands to expose edible crustaceans, worms, and mollusks.

*Passive—for now—
a pelican watches a
potential meal: a passing
galaxy of minnowlike
silversides off St. John's
North Shore.*

They are fairly young greens, all under two feet across. Hawksbills—the source of tortoiseshell—and the much rarer leatherbacks also occur in park waters. The greens move slowly but gracefully as they periodically dive to munch the sea grasses or surface for gulps of air.

Officially endangered or threatened in the U. S., all sea turtle species enjoy protection in St. John's waters. But just a few miles away, off the British Virgin Islands, turtle hunting remains legal. These three youngsters prove rather bold, calmly tolerating the strangers with glass faceplates even when they draw near. For several joyous moments the snorkelers tag after the reptiles, reveling in this chance wildlife encounter and feeling at one with the all-embracing sea. But then one pursues too closely or too quickly, and the turtles' sluggishness proves a sham; they increase their speed step for step with their followers and then—bored by the lack of challenge, perhaps—power out of sight.

Seconds later, a stingray three feet wide skims the sand floor, riding a thin seawater cushion like some alien hovercraft. Gill slits steadily pulse; the perimeter of its deltoid body gently undulates, stirring up sediments. Bulging, otherworldly eyes stare unblinkingly at their surroundings. The ray pauses, then scuds off, tailed by a lone bar jack nosing nonstop through its sandy wake, ever hoping for a meal among the debris.

Another North Shore site—this time, Maho Bay, east of Trunk—offers yet another habitat: Rocky ledges parallel the shore a few yards out, sheltering thousands upon thousands of gleaming minnows aptly named sil-

Graceful as it is tiny, the "cleaner" shrimp Periclimenes pedersoni *makes its home among the tentacles of an anemone in St. John's coral reefs, feeding on resident parasites.*

versides. Inch-long to anchovy-size, the fish array themselves in free-form curtains that waft to and fro like sequined drapes before a stage. Approach and the drapes momentarily part and rejoin, each minnow moving in concert as if it were merely one cell of a much larger superorganism, not an individual in its own right. Immature yellow-tail snappers, twice as big as the silversides but far fewer in number, drowsily school by, adding one more layer to the living veil.

In the blink of an eye, the curtains vanish. A dagger of molten silver—some four feet long and more streamlined than any shark—flashes onto center stage. It is all mouth and speed, the archetypal predator. Yet it makes not a single lunge at the thousands of potential snacks that by now have reformed their billowy curtains. Nor does it show any interest in sampling me, though it continues to stare my way for a long, long time. It's merely a curious barracuda.

Tarpon—some as long as myself—also patrol these waters, as do snook. They loom in and out of visibility, cruising slowly, without concern. Both species are highly prized sport fish, famed for striking fiercely and fast. But they too ignore the masses of silversides, which continue to ebb and flow, as regular as a metronome.

Then a sudden, foot-wide explosion of bubbles stabs down from above, instantly scattering the fingerlings. Slowly the froth clears, revealing here a webbed foot, there a rapier beak. A brown pelican, looking for lunch, has just dive-bombed the shallows. Feet paddle, wing tips splash, and soon the bird is airborne again, circling to make another pass at this ever movable feast.

Over and over I am struck by how quickly the shallows change from one ecosystem to another, each with its own complement of creatures. St. John's most dramatic under-sea attractions, however, lie beyond snorkeling range, in deeper waters accessible only with scuba gear. These are the fringing reefs, many of which front the island's eastern and southern shores, where volcanic bedrock has been worked into caves, steep ravines, even arches, then thickly encrusted with living facades.

Each stony coral species—and there are scores of them here—erects its own trademark topography, from mountainlike star corals to dwarf forests of elkhorn, from thin vanes of lettuce-leaf and plate corals to bulbous brains or brierlike thickets of staghorn. Knobby palisades of fire coral also rise up, as do black corals, sponges, anemones, and other sedentary sea life. Many divers find St. John's gorgonians—sea fans and sea whips—especially impressive. Within these dreamlike, otherworldly cities, free-form high-rises, crannied walls, and tangled staircases don't just harbor a dynamic and richly varied population, they're part of it.

Amid this fantastic stage swirls an equally fantastic cast of more mobile characters. A blaze of neon-orange spots marks a flamingo tongue—a tiny snail slowly rasping its way across a sea fan's lavender expanse. Stilt-legged shrimps and crabs hunker within the cavities of various cup sponges. One brain coral, big as a trophy pumpkin and probably into its third century of growth, sports a tassel of feathery, purple-and-white fronds nearly as big as my hand: feather duster worms.

Brilliant bits of magenta and yellow—fairy basslets—roam cave roofs upside down. Long, thin trumpetfish drift vertically, heads down, as they wait for prey to blunder near their siphonlike mouths. A lone trunkfish thrums stiffly by, its curveless profile all angles and straight lines, while iridescent, polygonal markings honeycomb its coppery skin. Three spiny lobsters, fearsomely armored with innu-merable sharp spikes, share a single pit in the coral wall. Blue tangs descend by the dozen to graze algae growing on a coral outcrop, then depart in a tight single file that slithers over the terrain like a long, segmented, blue worm.

A jut-jawed grouper patiently waits at a "cleaning station"

while tiny gobies pick parasites from its maroon-spotted body. French angelfish—each about a foot long by a foot wide but only half an inch thick—seem lately arrived from some two-dimensional realm. View them head-on and they very nearly disappear. But from the side, they glow; each black scale wears an edge of lurid, can't-miss yellow. If this animal's pancake shape is meant as camouflage, why the gaudy colors? A similar contradiction besets the peacock flounder stretched flat on a sand-filled ravine beneath me; while its ground color perfectly matches the sand, numerous electric-blue commas punctuate its body, grabbing my eye.

The reef's visual pleasures go on and on, always outlasting my air supply. There's such a congregation of life here, so many colorful and bizarre shapes, and all this magic lies so near shore, just 20 yards beneath the waves. Yet for many it remains forever out of sight, an invisible resource. Such "invisibility" is both a strength and a weakness, for while it helps shield the reef from heavy human traffic, it also ensures that when damage does occur, few notice.

Caroline Rogers, who is a reef ecologist, observes, "If someone goes out and bulldozes a redwood forest, lots of people are appalled. But if somebody drags an anchor through a reef, no one sees it—except for divers. It still looks beautiful from shore."

She speaks from experience. In 1988 a cruise ship accidentally dragged bottom west of Francis Bay, ripping a jagged swath through some 300 square yards of park-protected reef. While a suit filed by the Park Service has been settled, its details have not been released. In any event, Caroline sees no happy legal solution. "It's been really frustrating and challenging," she says. For one thing, no biologist enjoys reducing complex and dynamic natural systems to a bottom line. Also, she feels most people undervalue marine resources, simply because they don't see or know much about them.

"Over the last 20 years throughout the Caribbean," she adds, "there have been declines in the amount of living coral cover wherever it's been studied. A lot of places are going downhill." St. John's reefs "are in better shape than many others in the Caribbean, but they've also suffered. There have been serious decreases in some top predators and the more commercially important fish, such as groupers and snappers."

Often, causes are human-related: direct damage to reefs by boats and divers, overfishing, increased runoff due to spiraling onshore development. But nature also plays a role. Hurricane Hugo ravaged St. John in 1989, overturning and breaking numerous coral heads, smothering others with sediments. One reef, which Caroline and her research team had closely monitored before the storm, lost about 40 percent of its coral cover. Nine years later, she says, "There

has not been any significant recovery. I'm concerned about that. By far the most abundant coral there—*Montastrea annularis*—doesn't grow much more than a centimeter a year."

Even the Caribbean's slow-growing reefs, however, have managed to survive over centuries, despite innumerable hurricanes. What increasingly concerns scientists is that human-caused stresses such as overfishing and pollution may now be putting such pressures on reef systems that the added, occasional stress of a major hurricane simply pushes those reefs over the edge. They just can't recover as quickly or as completely as they once did. "Coral reefs are very complex, the most complex marine ecsytems you can look at," says Caroline. "They're very difficult to study."

In fact, scientific monitoring of coral reefs is fairly recent, going back about fourteen years on St. John. Humans, meanwhile, had been impacting reefs long before the first tour boats arrived. The plantation era showed no more respect for the island's reefs than it did the forests: Danish colonists regularly harvested brain corals for use as cornerstones and keystones in many plantation buildings, since corals were far more easily cut and shaped than the island's hard, volcanic rock. Visit any of the hundreds of Danish ruins that still litter St. John, and within their stone walls you're sure to find gleaming, sun-bleached coral blocks, as well as the thin clay bricks that came over as ships' ballast.

Moving tapestry of young French grunts illustrates a common defensive strategy on the reef: "predator swamping." By schooling densely, prey fish confuse would-be predators and increase their individual chances of survival.

Reef Bay Trail, which links the island's forested spine with its southern shore, follows plantation roads cobbled by Danish builders more than a century ago. I arrive just after a morning shower, the still-wet rocks agleam as sunlight filters through the broken canopy. Tiny lizards scamper, then freeze motionless. Dripping leaves and waterlogged trunks smell richly of life and decay, while trailside signs point out local sights.

Here are the dark, shiny leaves of bay rum or "wild cinnamon," once harvested and processed for the pungent oil that became bay rum cologne, a St. John specialty. There, a gumbo-limbo—also called "tourist tree" or "naked Indian"—bares its namesake, ever peeling red bark. Island-hopping Indians once worked the balsa-like wood of massive "elephant foot" trees into huge dugouts; Europeans used its fluffy seed-pod fibers to stuff pillows, mattresses, even life-jackets. They called the material "kapok."

Brown skeins of termite tunnels trace some trunks, connecting the insects' huge arboreal nests with the leaf-littered forest floor, where dead wood satisfies their nutritional needs. A golden-orb spider stands guard on a silken trap woven between giant anthurium leaves, waiting for a meal. Unseen doves call and rustle along the forest floor, while a whirr of wings signals the approach of a pearly-eyed thrasher. The barricade of trees thickens and rises as the trail descends; all is emerald, wild, primeval.

But then, jagged remnants of man-made walls jut through the green, stopping me dead. Vines, epiphytes, and who-knows-what clutter the stones, giving the impression of some wonderfully jungled Maya ruin. Living trees sprout from the very foundations. Decayed mortar, green with algae, barely reins in a tottering mix of field-stones, brain coral chunks, and ballast bricks that stairsteps upward in a would-be arch only to end in empty air. It is no Maya relic, of course, just part of an 18th-century sugar plantation. Yet it exudes the same mystique and mournful allure common to all ruins. Here, humans once lived and toiled; now they are gone. Nature is reclaiming her own.

Farther along, a side trail heads up a natural drainage, ending abruptly in a delightful little grotto. Two tannin-stained pools, set in black volcanic rock and fringed by razor grass, front a sheer wall of basalt some 40 feet high. The water is still, black, seemingly bottom-less, inhabited by tiny shrimp and a few water striders. Bright red dragonflies nearly as large as hummingbirds flush from the razor grass. Mosses, bromeliads, and other greenery spatter trees and even the rock wall, which trickles with the remains of this morning's rain. Standing water, *fresh* water, is unusual on St. John, which lacks the rainfall necessary to harbor even a single year-round river. Periodic downpours, however, turn this drainage into a temporary stream, the towering rock face into a waterfall—a dramatic gem of nature.

Yet most visitors come not for the grotto's natural attractions but for its man-made ones: A dozen or so petroglyphs, deeply incised into the hard rock, emblazon one pool's rim. They are bold and suggestive, magnetic in their starkness, like Matisse sketches. Most appear to be faces. One resembles a human skull, another an angry visage with flared brows. A third seems owl-like: Two huge eyes with tiny pupils stare from a heart-shaped faceplate. Yet another combines disk ears with a tiny, O-shaped mouth—the best of Minnie Mouse and Betty Boop? Some aborigine's image of God?

Sit a moment in this peaceful glade, let your fingers trace the channeled lines and dots, and ponder. Are these mere cartoons—or do they hold some yet-undeciphered message? Who made them? Why? Their creation demanded considerable effort, given the rock's hardness. Do even more lie hidden *below* waterline? Might this area's visual allure and rare store of freshwater once have served some social or even religious need for those who scratched the designs? History and science shed little light; different tales attribute this rock art variously to West African slaves or pre-Columbian Indians. The presence of an etched cross near the glyphs, some say, proves they are post-contact.

Park Service archaeologist Ken Wild remains unconvinced. "I think the glyphs are prehistoric," he says. "The cross shape has been associated with a number of pre-Columbian cultures, and similar crosses have been found in other areas of the Caribbean beside probable prehistoric petroglyphs." The most likely artists, he feels, are the ancestors of the Taino or the Taino themselves, the Indian culture that greeted Columbus in this area. That they lived here on St. John is known from various excavations and artifacts, which include zemi stones—three-pointed religious stones often engraved with effigy carvings. Recent finds of this culture are being studied by the National Park Service to enhance our understanding of these peoples. The artifacts are protected—but distant from their provenance.

Only the petroglyphs, which may or may not be Taino, remain here, open to view. I like the fact that in an age when it seems everything needs increased protection—biological resources, archaeological resources, even park visitors—you can still wander a park trail on your own, and experience the mystery and sense of discovery that comes with stumbling upon relics of a long-vanished society. There are no barricades here, no sterile display cases. The art remains accessible, intact, and enduringly real.

Like the numerous, scattered ruins of St. John's plantation era, the glyphs beckon with their starkness. They're just *there*, understated and totally exposed, in a lovely setting out at the edge of nowhere, waiting to be discovered and savored.

Rather like Virgin Islands National Park itself.

Gleaming vortex of silversides masks a light-wielding, nocturnal diver (opposite). The minnows draw other visitors as well, including a voracious pack of squids (below). Equipped with jet propulsion and ten tentacles each, these coppery torpedoes nimbly pursue and snare their prey. Huge eyes and extraordinary optic nerves enable these mollusks to navigate deftly even the darkest waters.

FOLLOWING PAGES: A fringe-headed blenny peeks out to find its reef home newly redone in mauve: Thousands of tiny eggs laid by a sergeant major— another reef-dwelling fish—now blanket the surface.

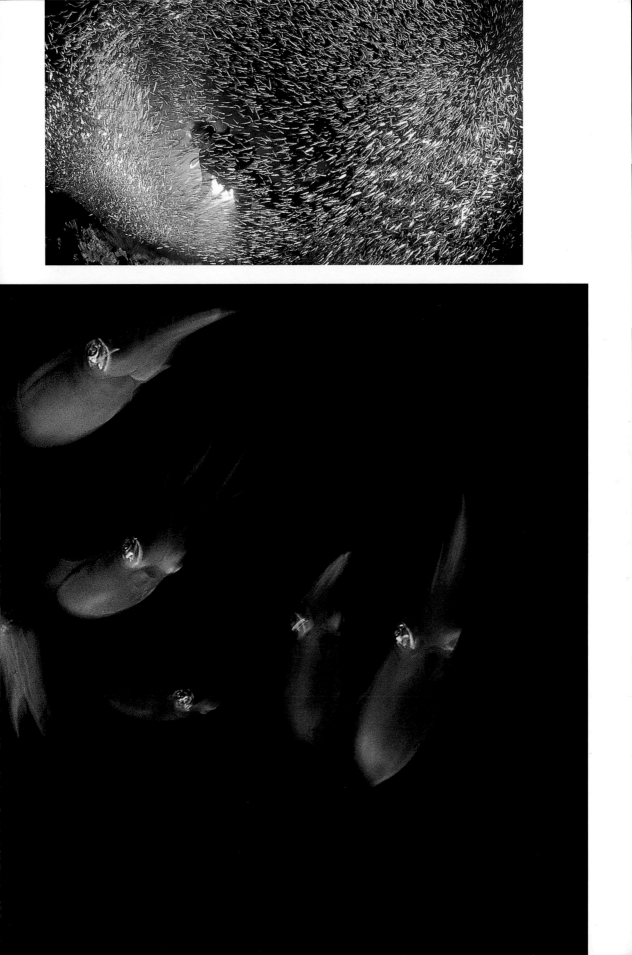

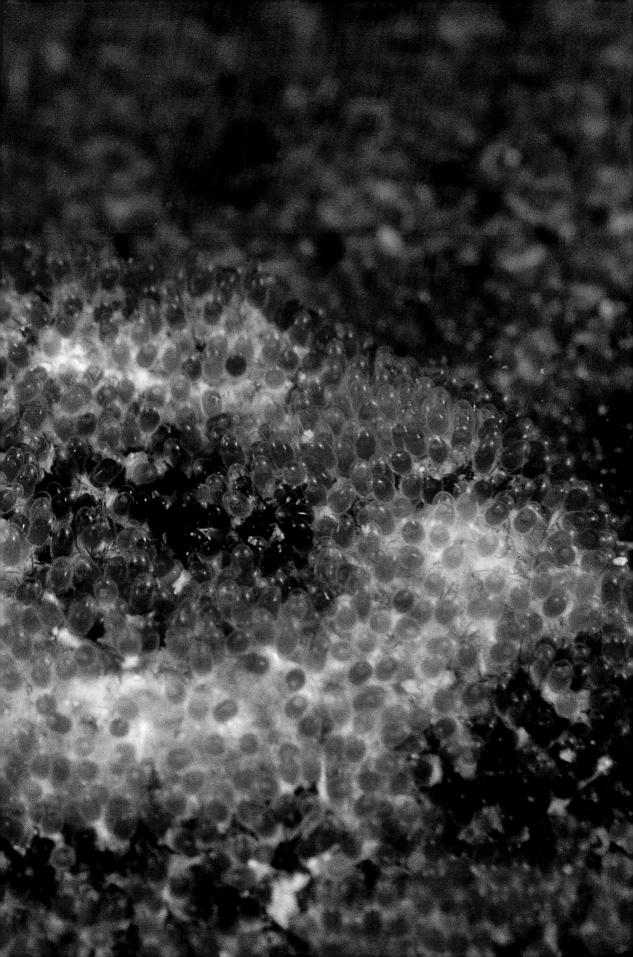

Rock garden of
Tubastrea, *a tube
coral, carpets an
undersea dropoff
(opposite). Its brilliant
yellow "blossoms,"
actually tentacles,
extend to immobilize
and ingest whatever
prey drifts by.
A trumpetfish hews
close to a sea fan's
living filigree (above).
Plantlike sea fans—* *soft corals—erect lacy,
flexible frameworks
mainly from protein
rather than from
limestone, as true
corals do. Wafting
with the currents,
the colonial, sedentary
animals help defuse
the sea's power, thus
minimizing storm and
wave damage to reefs.*

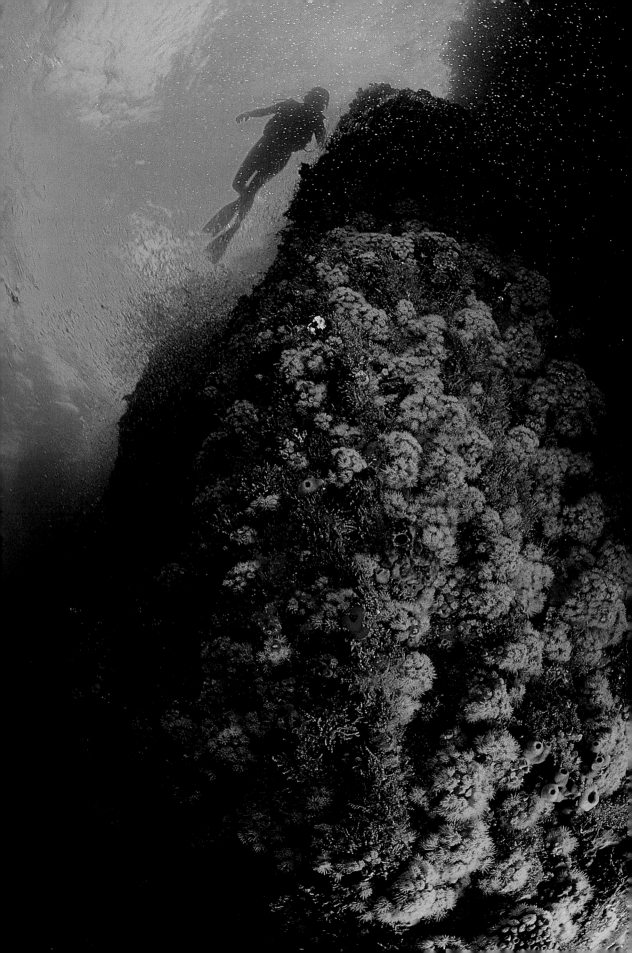

Grace notes from paradise: A drifting hibiscus blossom and Waterlemon Cay's ephemeral charms (below) affirm the enduring, Caribbean attraction of St. John and its national park.

Visiting
Virgin Islands

UNITED STATES VIRGIN ISLANDS
ESTABLISHED: August 2, 1956
SIZE: 12,909 acres (5,650 acres undersea)
HEADQUARTERS
6010 Estate Nazareth, St. Thomas
U. S. Virgin Islands 00802
Phone (340) 775-6238

HOW TO GET THERE
Commercial planes fly to Charlotte Amalie, capital of St. Thomas. You can take a public ferry from Charlotte Amalie (45 minutes), or from Red Hook (20 minutes), to Cruz Bay on St. John. You can also take a private boat. Some hotels provide free transfers between Charlotte Amalie and Cruz Bay.

WHEN TO GO
The park is open year-round. High season is from mid-December to mid-April, but the weather is stable most of the year, with daily temperatures averaging around 79°F.

GETTING AROUND
Ground transportation is needed between most hotels and beaches and other park attractions. Rental cars are available at several Cruz Bay locations (four-wheel-drive recommended), also taxicabs. Throughout the island, be prepared for steep roads with blind curves, and remember to *drive on the left.*

WHAT TO DO
The Visitor Center, located near the ferry dock at Cruz Bay, on St. John's western end, offers an informative video on the park, other displays, books, brochures, and information on current ranger-led activities.

If you have only one day, drive the **North Shore Road** from **Cruz Bay** as far as the **Annaberg**

Sugar Mill ruins, stopping at various beaches (perhaps to snorkel), such as **Trunk Bay**, **Cinnamon Bay**, **Maho Bay**, or **Waterlemon Cay**. At Annaberg, tour the various buildings of what once was a bustling sugar plantation.

Return via **Centerline Road**, stopping on Bordeaux Mountain for spectacular vistas of the island's **East End** (or for refreshment at the mountain's open-air restaurant). Turn off at

On a reach in deepening d

Catherineberg Road to visit the ruins of **Hammer Farm**, another 18th-century sugar mill that later was modified for the raising of lettuce.

Should you have more time, consider hiking **Reef Bay Trail**—just off **Centerline Road**—and seeing the **Petroglyphs**. Then explore the laid-back **East End** communities, such as **Coral Bay** and **Calabash Boom**, or take in the desertic beauty of **Saltpond Bay** and **Ram Head**.

SIDE TRIPS
Daily ferries run from Cruz Bay to nearby Tortola, in the British Virgin Islands. Be sure to bring your passport! Also, consider spending a day on St. Croix, USVI, just south of St. John. First sighted by Columbus, St. Croix boasts a historic site as well as Buck Island Reef National Monument, where underwater trails guide snorkelers and divers through the wonders of the coral reef.

l-trimmed yawl heads for the safe harbor of St. John's Hawksnest Bay.

DAVID ALAN HARVEY

NOTES ON CONTRIBUTORS

Chip Clark, a free-lance photographer based in Washington, D. C., has shot articles for NATIONAL GEOGRAPHIC TRAVELER. He has been exploring and photographing caves since he was in college.

Free-lance photographer **Jay Dickman,** who lives in Colorado, won a Pulitzer Prize in 1983 for his coverage of the war in El Salvador. He has contributed to Special Publications, including *America's Hidden Treasures: Exploring Our Little-Known National Parks,* and to NATIONAL GEOGRAPHIC.

David Doubilet, a contract photographer for National Geographic since 1977, has documented marine life from the Caribbean to New Guinea. He has taken photographs for chapters in several Special Publications and for more than 30 articles in NATIONAL GEOGRAPHIC. He is a lifelong resident of New York City.

As a staff member for more than 20 years, **Toni Eugene** wrote chapters for and edited numerous Special Publications and authored children's books and calendars. Since 1992 she has lived in Charlotte, North Carolina, where she is a free-lance editor and writer.

Contract photographer **Raymond Gehman,** a Virginia native, is covering national parks in Canada for an upcoming Special Publication. He photographed the earlier title *Yellowstone Country.*

Chris Johns, a free-lance photographer who lives in the Blue Ridge Mountains, shot the pictures for the Special Publication *Hawaii's Hidden Treasures.* He has contributed to NATIONAL GEOGRAPHIC and TRAVELER as well.

In the course of more than 25 years on staff, senior writer **Tom Melham** has visited nearly 50 national parks, from Zion to the Virgin Islands and from Gates of the Arctic to Big Bend. Numerous diving assignments have taken him to Lake Champlain, the Red Sea, Micronesia, and Australia.

Free-lance writer **Scott Thybony,** a resident of Flagstaff, Arizona, has explored national parks for previous Special Publications, including *Canyon Country Parklands,* and for *National Geographic's Guide to the National Parks of the United States.*

Former staff member **Jennifer C. Urquhart** found the Everglades fascinating and enjoyed the chance to revisit Biscayne, about which she had written in the Special Publication *America's Hidden Treasures.*

Mel White is a free-lance writer who lives in Little Rock, Arkansas, and specializes in travel and natural history. As a frequent contributor to TRAVELER, he has covered destinations from the Great Barrier Reef to the Amazon.

ACKNOWLEDGMENTS

The Book Division wishes to thank the individuals, groups, and organizations named or quoted in the text. In addition, we are grateful for the assistance of Tom Blount, Nancy Gray, Martha Hubbart, Steve Kemp, Joy Lyons, Rob Shanks, Joy Stiles, and Deborah Wade.

ADDITIONAL READING

The reader may wish to consult the *National Geographic Index* for related articles and books, in particular *National Geographic's Guide to the National Parks of the United States.* The following titles may also be of interest:

Acadia: Russell D. Butcher, *Field Guide to Acadia National Park, Maine*; Rachel Carson, *The Edge of the Sea*; Tammis E. Coffin, ed., *The Rusticator's Journal.* **Mammoth Cave:** Joy M. Lyons, *Mammoth Cave: The Story Behind the Scenery.* **Great Smoky Mountains & Shenandoah:** Rita Cantu, *Great Smoky Mountains: The Story Behind the Scenery*; John A. Conners, *Shenandoah National Park: An Interpretive Guide*; Henry Heatwole, *Guide to Shenandoah National Park*; Rose Houk, *Great Smoky Mountains National Park: A Natural History Guide.* **Biscayne:** Susan D. Jewell, *Exploring Wild South Florida*; L. Wayne Landrum, *Biscayne: The Story Behind the Scenery.* **Everglades:** Mark Derr, *Some Kind of Paradise*; Marjory Stoneman Douglas, *The Everglades: River of Grass*; Charlton W. Tebeau, *Man in the Everglades.* **Dry Tortugas:** Rodman Bethel, *A Slumbering Giant of the Past: Fort Jefferson, U.S.A. in the Dry Tortugas.* **Virgin Islands:** Eugene H. Kaplan, *A Field Guide to Coral Reefs*; Alan H. Robinson, *Virgin Islands National Park: The Story Behind the Scenery.*

Leaves of the staghorn sumac detonate in a burst of fall colors. As the season changes, the green chlorophyll in the plant fades and reveals the red and yellow pigments.

Index

Boldface indicates illustrations.

Acadia National Park, Me. **10-45**;
carriage roads 16-17, 29; coastline
18-19, **24-25**, 29-30, 40; fall foliage
41; maps 14-15; number of visitors
13; original name 13; rock climbing
28; size 13, 15; visitor information 45
Airboats 115, **136**, 140, 142
Ajax Reef, Biscayne National Park,
Fla.: submerged wreck **108-109**
Alicia (tramp steamer): wreck **108-
109**
Alligators **124-125**, 125, **134-135**;
ecological role 125, 134
Anemones 33, **180**
Angelfish, French 182
Anhinga Trail, Everglades National
Park, Fla. 115
Anhingas 115, **142**
Appalachian Trail, U. S. **80**, 83, 89
Arnold, Maj. Lewis G. 151-152
Audubon, John James: quoted on
Everglades 106, 143

Baker Island, Acadia National Park,
Me.: Gilley family cemetery 35
Bar Harbor, Me. 16, **20-21**
Barnacles 32
Bass Harbor Head Light, Acadia
National Park, Me. **44**
Bears, black **72**, **73**, 83, 91
Beech Mountain, Acadia National
Park, Me. **21**
Big Cypress National Preserve, Fla.
139-148; hunting ban 140; size 117,
142; visitor information 148
Big Meadows, Shenandoah National
Park, Va. **103**
Biscayne Bay, Fla. **111**; keys **111**
Biscayne National Park, Fla. **104-111**,
156; endangered species 106; light-
house **105**; map 110; shipwrecks 107,
108-109; size 104; visitor informa-
tion 110
Bleeding heart (plant) **75**
Blenny, fringe-headed **188**
Blindfish **52**, 53
Blue Ridge Parkway, Va.-N.C. 58, 99,
100-101
Boca Chita Key, Biscayne National
Park, Fla. **104-105**
Bone Valley, Great Smoky Mountains
National Park, N.C.-Tenn. 62

Bordeaux Mountains, St. John, U. S.
Virgin Islands 162
Bradley, Guy 117, 143
Brain coral **181**; plantation building
183, 184
Bromeliads **140-141**, **146-147**
Broward, Napoleon Bonaparte 119
Brown noddy terns **155**
Bubble Rock, Acadia National Park,
Me. 29
The Bubbles, Acadia National Park,
Me. 17, 29, **39**
Bunchberry **27**
Bush Key, Dry Tortugas National
Park, Fla.: sooty terns **152-153**

Cabbage palms **128**
Cactus, Turk's cap **172**
Cades Cove, Tenn. 58, 59, 63, 83; pio-
neer cabin **82**
Cadillac Mountain, Acadia National
Park, Me. 12, **40**; hikers **20-21**
Caneel Bay resort, St. John, U. S. Vir-
gin Islands 161
Caribbean region: coral reef decline
183-184
Carl Ross Key, Fla. 143; campers **126**
Carson, Rachel: quoted on tide pools
33
Caterpillar, frangipani **172**
Catfish, walking **142**
Caving **46-47**
Champlain, Samuel de 12, 20, 25
Charlies Bunion, Great Smoky Moun-
tains National Park, N.C.-Tenn. **76-
77**
Cherokee Indians 83, 84
Chestnut blight 89
Civil War, U. S. 62, 63, 151-152
Clingmans Dome, N.C.-Tenn. 62
Cobblestone Bridge, Acadia National
Park, Me. 31
Columbus, Christopher 161-162
Coral **108-109**, 156, 165, **181**; ancient
reef 106, **107**; damage 182, 183-184;
sea fans **106**, 190, **190**; tube coral
190, **191**
Corbin, George T. 90, 98
Corbin Cabin, Shenandoah National
Park, Va. 90, **98-99**
Crab, hermit **106**
Crayfish, blind **52**, 53
Crested dwarf iris **75**
Crickets: cave cricket **53**
Crocodiles, American **112**, 119
Croghan, Dr. John 50
Crystal Lake, Mammoth Cave,
Ky. 51, **54**, 55
Cypresses: bald cypresses 139,

140-141; dwarf cypresses 115

Deer, white-tailed **70-71**
Douglas, Marjory Stoneman **122**, 138;
quoted on Everglades 118, 119, 143
Dry Tortugas, Fla. 9; coral reefs 156;
migratory birds 155; name origin 153
Dry Tortugas National Park, Fla. **150-
157**; map 157; size 152-153; visitor
information 157
Duckweed **124**

Eagle Lake, Acadia National Park,
Me. 29, **38-39**
Eagles, bald 148, **149**
East Cape Sable, Florida Bay, Fla. **139**;
loggerhead sea turtle nesting area 139
The Edge of the Sea (Carson) 33
Egrets: great egrets **8**, **9**, 114, **128**;
snowy egrets 117
Everglades (region), Fla. 138; exotic
species 142, **142**; Indian name 118;
periphyton communities 133; water
management 118-119, 133, 136
Everglades Agricultural Area, Fla. 119,
138
Everglades National Park, Fla. **112-
149**; bald eagle nesting pairs 148;
decline in wading bird populations
118, 129, 133; endangered reptile
species 113; endangered status 118;
map 116-117; osprey population
decline 138; size 114, 117; visitor
information 148
The Everglades: River of Grass (Douglas) 118, 123

Florida Bay, Fla. 115, 117, **126-127**;
fishing decline 127; sea grass die-offs
118, 127
Florida panthers 139-140, 141-142
Flowstone: Mammoth Cave National
Park, Ky. 51, **54**
Fort Jefferson, Dry Tortugas, Fla.
150-153, **154-155**; nickname 150,
152
Frenchman Bay, Acadia National
Park, Me. **20-21**, 36
Friends of the Everglades 138
Frogging: Big Cypress National Pre-
serve, Fla. 142
Frogs: tree frogs **68**, 123
Frozen Niagara (flowstone), Mammoth
Cave National Park, Ky. 50
Fungi: destroying angel 37; fly amanita
mushrooms **37**

Genip **176-177**
Gilley, Joseph: grave 35

Gilley, William and Hannah 34
Golden-orb spiders **176,** 184
Granite, fractured **23**
Granite boulders **24-25**
Great Smoky Mountains National
  Park, N.C.-Tenn. **2-3,** 9, **56-85;**
  Civil War gravesites 62; fall foliage
  64-65, 78-79; forest **68-69, 80-81,**
  84-85; lumber industry 58, 62; map
  60-61; mountain people 59-61, 63,
  63, 83; name origin 57; precipitation
  84; salamander species 69; size 61;
  visitor information 102; visitors 58,
  61; white-tailed deer **70-71;** wildflower species 61, 75
Grunts, French **183**
Gumbo-limbos 115, 137, 184

Hammocks 115, 134, 137
Harebells **25**
Hawksbill Mountain, Shenandoah
  National Park, Va. 87-88
Hazel Creek, Great Smoky Mountains
  National Park, N.C.-Tenn. 61-63
Heads of the Martyrs (reefs), Florida
  Keys, Fla. 107
Heintooga Round Bottom Road,
  Great Smoky Mountains National
  Park, N.C.-Tenn. **78-79**
Herons, tricolored **129, 147**
Historic Entrance, Mammoth Cave
  National Park, Ky. 47, **48**
Hobblebush **27**
Hudson River school of art 16
Hurricane Andrew (1992): coral reef
  damage 108, 111; tree damage 106
Hurricane Hugo (1989): coral reef
  damage 182

Isle au Haut, Acadia National Park,
  Me. 15, 33-35

John Oliver family 83
Jordan Pond, Acadia National Park,
  Me. 17, **39**

Kapok trees 184
Kayaking **130-131**
Kephart, Horace 63, 82, 83
Kites: snail kites 143

Limeberry **176-177**
Limpets 32
Little Hunters Beach, Acadia
  National Park, Me. 22
Lobster boats **10-11**
Lobsters: catch 16, **17;** cooked 16
Loggerhead Key, Dry Tortugas
  National Park, Fla.: research lab

ruins **154**
Long Pond, Mount Desert Island, Me.
  21

Maho Bay, St. John, U. S. Virgin
  Islands 180
Mammoth Cave National Park, Ky.
  46-55; bat species 52; cutaway dia-
  gram of cave **48-51;** hospital 50-51;
  International Biosphere Reserve des-
  ignation (1990) 52; number of visi-
  tors 47; size 47, 53; visitor
  information 55; World Heritage Site
  designation (1981) 52
Mammoth Dome, Mammoth Cave
  National Park, Ky. 50
Mammoth Dome Sink, Mammoth
  Cave National Park, Ky. 53
Mangrove tunnels **130-131**
Mangroves, red **107,** 111, **112-113;**
  destruction by Hurricane Andrew
  106; nickname 106
Miccosukee Indians 136, **136,** 137
Millionaire's Row, Mount Desert
  Island, Me. 16, 17
Millipedes, African **176,** 177
Monkshood **35**
Moray eel, spotted **108**
Mosquitoes 137-138, 139
Mount Desert Island, Me.: Abnaki
  Indian name 39; cobblestones 23, **23;**
  cottagers 16; forest fire 17, 40; glacia-
  tion 17, 20, 29; name origin 12, 20
Mountain Green (farm), Shenandoah
  National Park, Va. 90-91
Mountain laurels **96-97**
Mudd, Dr. Samuel 156; memorial 152

Nicholson, Aaron 90
Nicholson Hollow, Shenandoah
  National Park, Va. 89, 90, **98-99**

Old Rag Mountain, Shenandoah
  National Park, Va. 85-86, **94-95**
Olmsted, Frederick Law, Jr. 30
Orchids: butterfly orchid **118;** *Oncid-
  ium variegatum* **177**
Osprey: feeding chick **138**
Otter Point, Acadia National Park,
  Me. **24-25,** 30; fishermen 30
Our Southern Highlanders (Kephart) 63

Palms: cabbage palms **128;** paurotis
  palms **124,** 125; sabal palms **140-
  141;** saw palmettos **128**
Palometas **158-159**
Park Loop Road, Acadia National
  Park, Me. 29-30
Parrotfish 165

Peace Hill, St. John, U. S. Virgin
  Islands: sugar mill ruins 175
Pelicans **179,** 181
Periwinkles 32
Petroglyphs **174-175,** 185
Pinestand Mountain, Shenandoah
  National Park, Va. **96-97**
Plume hunters: Everglades, Fla. 116-
  117, 133
Potomac Appalachian Trail Club 89,
  98
Proctor, Tenn. 62

Raccoon Oil Field, Big Cypress
  National Preserve, Fla. 141
Radiotracking: Florida panthers 139-
  140; red wolves 58, 66
Ram Head, Virgin Islands National
  Park, U. S. Virgin Islands **172-173**
Rat snakes, yellow 146, **146**
Red mangroves **107, 112-113;**
  destruction by Hurricane Andrew
  106, 111; nickname 106
Red reef hermit crab **106**
Red wolves 59, **67;** radiotracking 58,
  66
Reef Bay Trail, Virgin Islands
  National Park, U. S. Virgin Islands
  184
Rhododendrons **74**
River of Grass see Everglades
Roaring Fork, Great Smoky Moun-
  tains National Park, N.C.-Tenn. 78
Rock art: petroglyphs **174-175,** 185;
  stylized cross **175**
Rock climbing **28**
Rockefeller, John D., Jr.: parkland
  donation 16
Rockefeller, Laurance S. 161; parkland
  donation 160
Roseate spoonbills 114, 117, **132,** 133
Rotunda, Mammoth Cave National
  Park, Ky. 48, 49

St. John, U. S. Virgin Islands: Danish
  colonization 162, 175, 177, 183, 184;
  native tree species 177, 184; number
  of insect species 164; plant species
  161; rare and endangered plants 164;
  second-growth forest **176-177;** size
  160; subtropical moist forest 162-
  164; sugar plantation ruins 175, 184;
  tropical dry forest 164-165; warbler
  species 164-165
Salamander, cave **69**
Sand Beach, Acadia National Park,
  Me. 29, **42-43**
Saw grass 114, 118, **122,** 123, **123,**
  144-145

Saw palmettos **128**

Schoodic Peninsula, Acadia National Park, Me. 13, 15, **36**

Scott Bay, St. John, U. S. Virgin Islands: sea turtles 165, 180

Sea fans 106, 190, **190**

Sea squirts 165

Sea turtles 139, 156, 165, 180

Seal Harbor, Mount Desert Island, Me. **10-11**

Sergeant major: eggs **188-189**

Shark River, Everglades National Park, Fla.: bird life 137

Shark River Slough, Everglades National Park, Fla. 114

Sheep Porcupine Island, Acadia National Park, Me. **20-21**

Shenandoah National Park, Va. **1**, 9, **85-103**; apple-growing 90-91; black bear population 91; ferns 93, **93**; maps 86-87; tree species 87, 89; visitor information 102-103; visitors 87, 88; white-tailed deer population 90; wildflower species 96

Shrimp, cleaner (*Periclimenes pedersoni*) 180

Silversides **178-179**, 180, **187**

Skiffs, glade **120-121**

Skyline Drive, Shenandoah National Park, Va. 87, 89

Slash pines 115, **128**, **134**; decimation by Hurricane Andrew 134

Snails: apple snails 143; tree snails 139

Snakes: rat snake **146**; water moccasin **145**

Somes Sound, Mount Desert Island, Me. 15, 17, 29

South Florida Natural Resources Center 133

Spence Field, Great Smoky Mountains National Park, N.C.-Tenn. 83

Spiders, golden-orb **176**, 184

Spiderwort **96**

Split-rail fences **99**

Spoonbills, roseate 114, 117, **132**, 133

Spruce trees **18-19**, **26**, **80-81**

Squids 186, **186-187**

Stingrays **178**, 180

Storks: wood storks 118, 133

Sugar plantations 177, 184; mill ruins **175**

Taino Indians 175, 185

The Tempest (Shakespeare) 107

Terns: brown noddy terns **155**, 156; sooty terns **152-153**, 156

Thunder Hole, Acadia National Park, Me. 30

Tide pools 23, 31-33

Tree frogs 68, 123

Tricolored herons **129**, 147

Troglobites 52, 53; number of species unique to Mammoth Cave 53

Trogloxenes 52

Trumpetfish 181, **190**

Trunk Bay, St. John, U. S. Virgin Islands 165, **168-169**, **170-171**; underwater trail 165, **168**

Tunicates 165

Turkey Point, Everglades, Fla.: crocodile breeding habitat 118, **119**

United States: map of eastern seaboard 7

Virgin Islands National Park, U. S. Virgin Islands **4-5**, **158-195**; coral reef life 165, **165**, **168**, **180**, 180-182; establishment 160; map 162-163; rock art **174-175**, 185; size 163; visitor information 194-195

Walking catfish **142**

Water moccasin (snake) **145**

Waterlemon Cay, St. John, U. S. Virgin Islands 192-193

Whiteoak Canyon, Shenandoah National Park, Va. **92**

Wild rose 39

Wild strawberry **84**

Willoughby, Hugh L. 135

Yawl: St. John, U. S. Virgin Islands 195

Zemi stones 185

Guide to Park Symbols

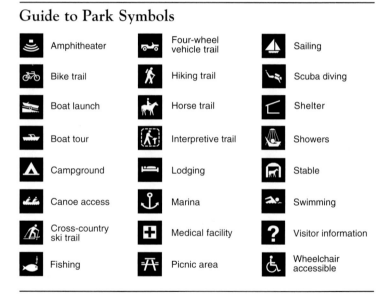

Amphitheater

Bike trail

Boat launch

Boat tour

Campground

Canoe access

Cross-country ski trail

Fishing

Four-wheel vehicle trail

Hiking trail

Horse trail

Interpretive trail

Lodging

Marina

Medical facility

Picnic area

Sailing

Scuba diving

Shelter

Showers

Stable

Swimming

Visitor information

Wheelchair accessible

Library of Congress CIP Data

Our inviting Eastern parklands / prepared by the Book Division, National Geographic Society, Washington, D. C.
    p.   cm.
    Includes index.
    ISBN 0-87044-978-8
    1. National parks and reserves—East (U. S.) 2. National parks and reserves—East (U. S.)—Pictorial works.   I. National Geographic Society (U. S.). Book Division.
E160.09 1994
974—dc20   94-19638
                                                                                                          CIP

Composition for this book by the National Geographic Society Book Division. Set in Goudy. Map production by GeoSystems, Lancaster, Pa. Color separations by Digital Color Image, Cherry Hill, N.J.; Graphic Art Service, Inc., Nashville, Tenn.; Lanman Progressive Co., Washington, D. C.; Lincoln Graphics, Inc., Cherry Hill, N.J.; Penn Colour Graphics, Inc., Huntingdon Valley, Pa.; Phototype Color Graphics, Pennsauken, N.J. Printed and bound by R. R. Donnelley & Sons, Willard, Ohio. Dust jacket printed by Miken Systems, Inc., Cheektowaga, N.Y.